Ivy Williams

Ivy Williams

Ivy Williams
"Byw Yr Ydwyf Trwy Ffydd"
("I live by faith")

Bridget Wheeler

WOODBRIDGE
PUBLISHERS

ISBN – 979-8-9860447-3-6 – (Hardback)

Published by Woodbridge Publishing

Leeds, UK

woodbridgepublishers.co.uk

Phone: +44-113-4900-487

Table of Contents

A word from my sponsors

The partners at Wordley Partnership are pleased to support this book, which celebrates the achievements of Ivy Williams, who 100 years ago realised her dream of becoming a barrister in times when not only were women discriminated against by law and society at large but also by the male judiciary who persistently refused to accept a woman as a barrister.

We do so in recognition of the increasingly leading role that women occupy in the legal landscape today but with still much to do. We also realise that in understanding the struggle of Ivy Williams, a woman of immense courage, we task ourselves with promoting diversity in our own workplace.

We hope that this book will inspire those starting out on a legal career and remind us that although things have changed, there is still some way to go. Wordley Partnership aspires to promote a vision of a legal profession where Ivy's legacy will continue to clear the way for everyone to be judged by their abilities and nothing else. We hope that this book will act as a guide as well as a description of the life of an extraordinary woman who refused to bow to prejudice to prevent her from achieving her rightful place at the Bar.

Wordley Partnership 2022

Foreword

One hundred years since women were admitted to the Bar is the right time to pay respect to Ivy Williams – respect and gratitude denied her in her lifetime. I studied law at her college, St Anne's Oxford University (then called the Home –Students), and subsequently spent many years there as the law tutor and then the Principal (1970 –2004). Law studies at the college were steeped in her legacy, and her photograph is hung in the Geldart Law Library, one of the best of college law libraries in Oxford. Her works on the Swiss Civil Code are preserved there. I met her fleetingly during my undergraduate years but was unaware then of just how much she should have meant to me. I will always regret not having thanked her, and in some small measure, my contribution to this interesting biography may make amends.

Ivy's father was a solicitor of 12 King Edward Street, Oxford, coincidentally the location of my husband's solicitors' firm until 1996. Ivy joined the Home –Students in 1896 and had the good fortune to be taught by Edward Jenks and W S Holdsworth. She was to become the first woman to teach law at an English University, as well as being a trailblazer in being called to the Bar. Her brother, Winter, was also called to the Bar before dying tragically young. In his memory, she endowed a generous scholarship for law students at Oxford, which continues to this day.

Ivy was some considerable scholar. Not only the BA but the BCL, a London LLD and eventually an Oxford DCL, the highest law degree that there is was given in recognition of her work on the Swiss Civil Code.

Professor Geldart, the holder of the Vinerian Chair of English Law, successor to Dicey, had encouraged her to take up this topic, and to this day, she is remembered by Swiss legal scholars for her work. In 1920, the year that women were first admitted to the Inns of Court, Ivy was admitted to the Inner Temple, sponsored by Sir John Simon. She was called to the Bar in 1922, having taken a First in the Bar examinations. She was the first woman to be called to the Bar and was called by the son of Charles Dickens, Sir Henry Dickens.

As early as 1904, Ivy had called for women to be allowed to practise law. The Law Journal noted that she had said: "Ladies holding University law degrees, learned and skilled in the law, deservedly enjoying public confidence, could legally compete in vast fields of solicitor's and counsel's most lucrative domains and without infringing the law." Nevertheless, the prejudice remained. Noting her call in 1922 the Law Journal editorialised about the difficulties "which are almost certain to arise if [women] engage in the conflict of the Courts, especially in cases in which the less prudent of them may deem themselves to be peculiarly qualified to appear by reasons of their sex. Their admission to the Bar ... is never likely to be justified by any success they will achieve in the field of advocacy."

In her mid –40s by then, Ivy did not practise but became a Tutor in Law from 1920 –45 and dedicated herself to the advancement of women in their career and as law students, a tradition strongly upheld by her college, St Anne's. Most of the women studying law at Oxford in those 25 years were taught by her, as there were hardly any other law tutors in the women's colleges.

When in later life, her eyesight began to fail, Ivy once more turned adversity to great use: she systematised Braille, taught others and published a Braille primer. Former pupils admired her kindness and courage. The continuing general reluctance to accept women into the legal profession saddened her. She died in Oxford in 1966. She did not live to see the tremendous advances made by women lawyers shortly thereafter. Today no doubt, she would have been a QC and a professor; but her input enabled others to rise to those ranks. Those who knew her admired her greatly, and all of us should be grateful to her for showing the way to the promised land.

Baroness Ruth Deech QC (Hon)

Prologue

Ivy Williams is best known for being the first woman in England and Wales to be called to the Bar. She is also my cousin twice removed and hard to pin down.

Ivy was a personal inspiration through her reputation within the family and as a pioneer for women. She is the reason I read law and the reason I went to the Bar myself. But I knew very little about her. By the time I started to take a deep interest in her story, almost everyone who had known her was no more. My investigation was a patchwork of searching the internet, combing through newspaper archives, taking tea with my aunt and going through papers that she had saved from destruction, and reaching out to the institutions where she had left her mark. And as I searched, things fell slowly into perspective, anomalies tended to be resolved, and she started to emerge from the (often scant) data.

Apart from Ivy's well documented and publicised call to the Bar and her academic achievements, she has left little trace of her personal life. She never married and on the whole such papers as she left are no more. Many of her wide family also remained unmarried, and two world wars diverted what might have been a very different career into one of public service and support for others. She became, through circumstances, a gentle disrupter rather than the trail blazer she promised in her youth. I have been fortunate in having that remnant of family papers to throw some further light on this quiet and retiring woman, which, together with the now freely available public domain information and the work done by others, allows us to see more.

This is Ivy's story.

Not just a footnote in the drive over the last century for a voice in the legal world for women of all backgrounds – but a true enabler.

It is also a story of women. Women emerging from their former traditional roles as mothers and wives; women stepping into the centre. Ivy's family were firm feminists. She had never to fight against tradition within her own domestic circumstances; rather, as she said on the night of her eventual call to the Bar, her call fulfilled a dream that she and her father shared for her, and earlier in her life, she explained that *"[she had] been educated expressly for the legal profession"*. In short, it was a team effort.

And what a team. Granddaughter of Gladstone's one – time parliamentary agent, with an entrepreneurial father and brother, the entire family Liberal activists; cousins who were amongst the first women doctors and who answered the call of the missionary to serve in places far from the family home in Oxford, who saw slavery with their own eyes and railed against it. Cousins who were close to her, with whom she maintained a correspondence. Cousins who did extraordinary things. A family who, by a large, she outlived by many years, her earlier years of family duty giving way to later years of solid academia and mentoring of other young women.

In spite of everything, she was not a suffragette in the traditional mould. But a friend and ally of the women who marched and protested.

Finding Ivy has led me down many interesting paths and to sources I never expected to find. I discovered a strong –minded woman, fierce in her beliefs, determined in her ambition, shy but accomplished as a public speaker. A woman of whom former pupils spoke fondly. A woman who gave much to her local community and, in particular, to the cause of women. A woman who probably sacrificed a more active role for family duty. Someone who was uniquely blessed with the circumstances in which she grew up and who was able to grasp with both hands when the time was right her place in legal history. This year marks 100 years after her milestone call to the Bar seemed to me to be the right time to shine a light on her life.

Bridget Wheeler

Sandon, Hertfordshire

Chapter 1
The Oxford connection

In pulling together the information available privately and publicly, I have wondered what it is that brings together all the elements necessary to produce a pioneer of great intellect for whom things all fall into place.

The genetic code no doubt plays a part in the circumstances into which the person is born, the upbringing, education, and the world events. But sometimes these polarise in a striking way when added into the mix are close relatives of brilliant ability and great personal bravery, also pioneers in their own right, a hugely supportive and early feminist family well able to fund education. And to be brought up in Oxford, at a time when women were making their mark – at last –was perhaps the biggest advantage of all.

Oxford University had been an almost monastic establishment until 1877. Up until that time, all teachers and candidates for admission were male, and university fellows were forbidden to marry. Women did not take degrees until 1920. However, there were early rumblings: "Examinations for women" were first set up in 1875, and an early candidate achieved a first in 1877. The first Women's college was established in 1879.

1877 bought with it a change of attitude. With the University Reform Act 1877 abolishing the requirement for chastity, suddenly, fellows were permitted to have wives and families. To some extent, this led to the building of large family houses, an influx of women and a baby boom. Ivy Williams was born in 1877 in that iconic year, and although (as described below) she was born in Newton Abbot, Ivy was to return with her family to an Oxford that was fast changing as a young child of an affluent and influential family.

I am indebted to the University of Oxford and, in particular, Alexandra Hughes –Johnson for allowing me to "borrow" (and slightly edit) their summary of the arrival and progress of women at Oxford, which in turn owes much to that definitive review, "The Women at Oxford; a Fragment of History" by Vera Brittain.

> *"[Women] had been making their mark on the University and advocating for women's access to an Oxford education since the 1860s. The Delegacy of Local Examinations opened local exams to schoolgirls in 1870 (after refusing to do so in 1862 and 1866), but higher local examinations were not open to women over the age of eighteen until 1875. By this time, a successful lecture scheme for women was available, having been founded in 1873.*
>
> *'Lectures for Ladies', as the scheme became known, was convened by an informal committee of dons' wives and sisters which included Mary Humphry Ward, Louise Creighton, Charlotte*

14

Green and [of significance for Ivy] Bertha
Johnson [who ran the Society of Home –Students
which Ivy was to join (later St Anne's)]. The
reform –minded women secured prominent
scholars including Arthur Johnson, Mark
Pattison and William Sedgewick to deliver
lectures to a number of interested women.[1] The
scheme continued for six years, with lectures
taking place in a room in the Clarendon Building.

The foundation of the women's halls

These informal lectures for women were part of a
nationwide movement for women's access to
higher education and helped stimulate serious
discussion in Oxford about establishing a small
hall of residence for women ... Girton College
had opened in 1869 and the entrance of women
into an all –male Cambridge environment
suggested that successful integration was
possible.[2] In fact, it was after a visit to Girton in
1878, that Edward Talbot (Warden of Keble) and
Lavinia Talbot, chaired a meeting in Keble
College, on the 4 June 1878, where it was decided
that an Anglican women's hall of residence

---

[1] Brittain, *The Women at Oxford*, 44 –46. Judy Batson, *Her Oxford*, 19. A similar scheme was established by Eleanor Smith in 1866 but this was less successful due to a lack of support from male dons and a limited number of women at Oxford during this period.
[2] Janet Howarth, 'In Oxford but ... not of Oxford', 244 –246.

*should be established in Oxford.[3] Oxford's first
women's higher education institution was named
Lady Margaret Hall (after Lady Margaret
Beaufort) and its first Principal was Elizabeth
Wordsworth. While LMH was founded in 1878, it
opened in October 1879 in Norham Gardens with
just nine students. At the same time, Somerville
Hall (named after the mathematician, Mary
Somerville) was established as a non –
denominational institution. Somerville opened on
the Woodstock Road with twelve students, under
the leadership of its Principal, Madeleine Shaw
Lefevre.*

*Somerville Hall and LMH operated for many
years as residential halls. Educational provision
for their students was organised by a separate,
centralised organisation established in June
1878, the Association for Promoting the Higher
Education of Women (more commonly known as
the AEW). While the AEW had no legal or
statutory status in relation to the University, the
institution collected fees for lectures, organised
tutorials and lectures, hired tutors and enforced
various rules and regulations. While the
Association's centralised role in providing tutors
was soon challenged by women's societies such
as Somerville, which proposed employing its own
residential tutors, the AEW remained an
important link between the women's Halls and*

---

[3] LMH Council Minute Book, 1878 –1884. As quoted in Howarth, 'In Oxford
but … not of Oxford', 256.

16

the wider University.[4] *The AEW was also the parent –body which oversaw the Oxford Home – Students, the name given to women students residing in family homes or as lodgers in the homes of 'hostesses' in Oxford, rather than in halls. In 1879, The Society for Oxford Home – Students (formally named as such in 1898) had twenty –five women students who were welcomed under the supervision of the Lady Secretary of the AEW. Initially, this was Charlotte Green, who was followed by Bertha Johnson in 1893. The Society for Oxford Home –Students would eventually become what we know today as St Anne's College.*

By 1893, two further women's halls had been established. St Hugh's Hall was founded in 1886 by Elizabeth Wordsworth as an institution for women who couldn't afford the fees at LMH and Somerville. St Hugh's (named after St Hugh of Avalon) offered lower fees, with economy being achieved by frugal living and smaller accommodation. Charlotte (Annie) Moberly was St Hugh's first Principal and she opened the Hall with just four students. St Hugh's was followed by St Hilda's Hall. St Hilda's (named after St Hilda, head of Whitby Abbey) was founded by the Principal of Cheltenham Ladies College, Dorothea Beale, with the primary intention of housing pupils from Cheltenham Ladies College.

---

[4] Janet Howarth, 'In Oxford but ... not of Oxford', 249.

17

Beale appointed Esther Burrows as the first Principal of the Hall, which opened with seven students in 1893.

The move for women's degrees

As the women's halls and societies developed and expanded, the question of opening degrees for women began to surface. This, in tandem with the recommendation by a Royal Commission that Scottish universities should open their degrees to women, meant that by 1895 Oxford and Cambridge were the only British universities to deny women degrees. Women were allowed to take all the examinations leading to the BA degree at Oxford, but while they laboured under almost the same conditions as the men, they had little to show for their efforts by the time they left the university. Consequently, pro and anti – degree debates ensued and the Hebdomadal Council was petitioned by educational reformers and members of the University who demanded that women receive recognition for their efforts. All petitions and proposed resolutions to the university statutes were denied in the first move for degrees in 1896. Women continued to be regarded at best as 'honoured guests' in a university which remained unsure about their status.[5]

A Delegacy for Women Students was established in November 1910, marking a new and important phase of the campaign for women's education in Oxford. It had been prompted by HT Gerrans' (Secretary of the Oxford Delegacy for Local Examinations and Tutor of Maths at Worcester College) suggestion to the Hebdomadal Council that women should be recognised as members of the university and that the university should itself formally assume supervision and control of them. The university's formal approval of the Delegacy for Women Students was a huge step towards women's full membership of the university, not least because the statute which established the Delegacy acknowledged women as university members for the first time. In November 1910, a writer to The Times *reflected on women's progress, stating:*

'Oxford has recognised that she has daughters, and some day she will give to them, as to her sons, the right to bear her name and wear her gown'.[6]

[5] Batson, *Her Oxford*, 110 –111.
[6] Brittain, *The Women at Oxford,* 132.

1920 ceremonies

Nonetheless, it took another ten years for women to be recognised as full members of the university, as it wasn't until October 1920 that women matriculated and were awarded degrees for the first time. On 7 October 1920, the matriculation of the first 130 women students took place in the Divinity School. A report of the day in the Oxford Times *recalled that 'the Divinity School was alive with trim figures in cap and gown in various stages of excitement, all carrying the university statute book under their arms and all proud of their newly –won distinction'.[7] Speaking directly to her students outside the Divinity School, the Principal of LMH, Henrietta Jex Blake, proclaimed 'this is the proudest day of my life – you are historic characters – the first women ever matriculated in this leading university of the world'.[8]*

The first –degree ceremony followed at the Sheldonian Theatre on 14 October 1920. Among those who received their degrees on this date were the Principals of the women's colleges, former students, women tutors and administrators, and women prominent in the educational and reform movements in the nineteenth and twentieth centuries. During 1920

[7] *The Oxford Times*, 'Daughters of the University', October 8, 1920.
[8] Batson, *Her Oxford*, 189.

and 1921, a total of 1159 women matriculated. Eleanor Lodge summarised the feeling of many of these women:

'Only those who have lived by the university but not of it, who have done university work but without being university members, can fully appreciate the vast difference it makes to be now at last part of the great institution, which has been so long the home of students and scholars.'[9]

While 1920 was a momentous landmark in the history of women's education in Oxford, it was not until 1957 that the quotas restricting the number of women undergraduates were finally removed. Likewise, it was only in 1959 that the five women's colleges received the same 'full status' as the men's colleges, and their Heads became eligible to become Vice –Chancellor. In 1961, Lucy Sutherland became the first woman Pro –Vice –Chancellor and the Oxford Union extended full membership to women. Yet, it took until 2015 for Professor Louise Richardson to become the first woman in the history of the university to become Vice –Chancellor. She became the 272nd VC, breaking an 800 –year pattern of male leadership."

Oxford had become a city in 1542, but the origins of modern–day Oxford date in the main from around 1771, with the establishment of the Paving Commission and Board of Guardians taking responsibility for development

---

[9] Bailey, *Lady Margaret Hall*, 90.

and welfare. Ivy's grandfather Adin was a member of both institutions. The population in 1772 was around 9,500, with university students numbering less than 3,000. There was little population increase until the 1800s when a surge occurred between 1811 and 1831. The city lacked, however, an industrial base to sustain greater population movement until the advent of the car industry in Cowley and the corresponding development of the area between 1910 and 1930. On the tail end of this surge in the 1820s, the Williams family moved into the city.

By the latter part of the nineteenth century, boundary extensions had created *"[an] elite of prosperous townsmen. Characterised by small tradesmen, craftsmen and college servant ... a wide gap between rich and poor ... rows and courts of squalid and insanitary cottages [at St Aldates] ... [regular cholera outbreaks] and notorious rowdiness and corruption of parliamentary elections in Oxford."* Poverty was lessened by voluntary charitable donations, and there was a serious underemployment problem with the university only being in residence for half of the year: *"the wealthy men of Oxford were brewers, bankers, lawyers, newspaper proprietors and clothiers".*

Against this melee, the Paving Commission started to plan for the needs of the modern city. Uncontrolled flooding of areas of the city led to regular outbreaks of cholera which would remain until the basic infrastructure was addressed. Towards the end of the eighteenth century, widespread demolition of the east and north gates and the Bocardo took place. This was followed by the demolition of Butchers shambles, poor housing in Queen Street and part of Butterbench in Carfax. Magdalene bridge was rebuilt, and the new road to Henley (Iffley Road) was built. The outdoor market was replaced with an indoor market, and restrictions started to be imposed on protruding signage. High Street paving was completed in 1779. In 1834, whilst Summertown was beginning to be established as an out –of –town Georgian village, a row of buildings at St Aldates was destroyed; St Clements church was demolished in 1830.

Oxford had acquired a canal in 1790 and a railway in 1844, although from 1838 the line to London had reached Steventon to the west of Didcot, putting it within reach of Oxford travellers. Initially opposed due to some insensitive initial planning of the routeway and concerns by the university for the morals of the students allowed to visit London so easily, such fears had subsided by 1842, and the routeway was opened.

So, whilst it is tempting to think that it was the abolition of the requirement of celibacy for university lecturers in 1877 that led to a boom in family housing, in fact, the development of the town was already proceeding under the newly established commissions. For example, by 1877, much of north Oxford had already been developed, with the early development of Summertown in 1830 having been followed by infilling that linked it to the city. Undergraduates had been allowed to live out of college since 1868, creating a need for lodgings in the city.

In short, by the time of Ivy's family's arrival back in Oxford in the 1880s, the city was reinventing itself, and the men of business (i.e. Ivy's family) were dominant drivers in that enterprise. Cowley was about to explode as an industrial area, and of interest is that the family – initially based in central and northern Oxford and always favouring new builds – invested in that area and, in due course, moved there.

Chapter 2
The move to Oxford

Ivy's grandmother Eliza Williams (nee

Bolton) in old age

Ivy's grandfather, Adin Williams, who brought the family into Oxford and away from their farming roots in nearby Cote, Shifford and Bampton

It was Ivy's grandfather Adin (1803 –1876) who brought the family into Oxford.

Adin was one of nine children of Peter and Ruth (nee Collett) Williams of Old Shifford Farm, located near Cote and Bampton to the north of Oxford. The children's births are variously recorded as taking place in Cote or Aston, both small settlements close to Old Shifford Farm. The 1851 Census records the family as fairly substantial farmers, Old Shifford Farm being adjacent to New Shifford Farm, which was owned by the Wallis family, said to be cousins of the Williams. Of the nine children, only five survived into adulthood, and Adin was something of a "rainbow" child, having been born shortly after the death of his young brother Ebenezer. Only his younger brother Richard survived Adin and lived long enough to have met Ivy. Richard died in 1884 in Kingston Road, Oxford, having it seems moved into the city at some stage prior to his death.

Adin's parents had a close and happy marriage before the untimely death of Ruth, aged 34, when Adin was 8. His father never remarried.

The Williams siblings all maintained close ties with Cote, where they worshipped in the chapel. The graveyard there is full of substantial monuments to Williams brethren (and sometimes their wives). Letters from Ivy's solicitor and cousin, Percy Prior, suggest that Ivy and her then housekeeper "Miss Jackson" still retained property in Cote (of which Miss Jackson was extremely proud) in the 1920s; however, in context, this seems in fact to be a reference to the house that Ivy moved into in the latter part of her life in Staverton Road, Oxford, which she named "Cote" in remembrance of her family's origins. Of Adin's surviving siblings, all (with the possible exception of his older brother Boaz) seem to have remained in the locality – as had generations before them – firmly grounded in rural agricultural life in Old Shifford. His other brothers worked the farm, and his sister Abigail married the next – door farmer and cousin, William Talbot Wallis. The Wallis children seem to have socialised closely with those of Adin. Within their own circle, there were at least six instances of intermarriage between the local families of Williams and Collett: Adin's mother, for example, was the daughter of the much –respected Reverend Collett,

27

and in 1960 Ivy was to leave a bequest to her friend and helper "Mrs Collett".

The family were not, however, inward –looking or narrow –minded in their outlook. They had prospered (by and large) from hard work and took positions of responsibility within their church and village. They were benefactors to the Congregationalist church. For example, the 1742 Aston Commons Book records the names of members of "the Sixteen"; these were villagers elected to oversee the organisation of agriculture in the parish, all but two of whom were sufficiently literate to sign their own names. The Williams family are prominent amongst the Sixteen, the list including John Williams Junior, Adin Williams, Adin Williams younger, Ebenezer Williams and John Williams.

Education in the vicinity had been formalised in 1709 with the establishment locally of a charity for education, which continued to fund local education until 1856 when a National School was established at Aston. In addition, there were local Dame's schools, one of which seems to have been at Aston West End, at Sauceroy House. It is unlikely that Adin and his siblings attended these schools. Whilst there is no suggestion of any Oxfordshire Williams attending Oxford University until Ivy's generation, wealthier families did educate their children privately at home. There was a grammar school in Bampton endowed by Robert Versey of Chimney, another at Witney and a dissenting school built at Aston in 1827 run by the Baptists. By 1845 this had become known as the British School and was established in a building in North Street Aston; it was also used for religious services. Alongside the nonconformist school, the church school was established in 1857.

Adin's early education was unlikely to have taken place at a local school. By the time he was of school age, the school at Bampton had ceased to offer a "Classical" education and was having trouble attracting a graduate as a teacher. Adin's will emphasises the importance he placed on education, and whether this is because he felt that he lacked the advantages he saw on his move to Oxford or whether it reflects his own happy experiences is hard to say. Adin seems to have been highly literate, and his handwriting is well –formed and would suggest, at the very least, a fairly thorough educational grounding.

The Williams' farmland was extensive at a time when agricultural work was labour intensive and required many hands to work it, but it may be that as the third son, Adin felt that he should seek his fortune elsewhere. Certainly, his activities once he settled in Oxford confirm that he was a man of intelligence, ambition and firmly held views that he was not afraid to express and a shrewd and successful businessman. By the latest, the end of 1828, he was residing in Oxford. The indications are that he started off as a mercer's assistance at 136, High Street and later took over the shop. Whilst this was almost certainly initially as a tenant, his will discloses that by his death he had acquired the freehold to that address.

Adin's removal to Oxford may have had something to do with his marriage to the Bolton family of nearby Cumnor. He married Eliza Bolton, the daughter of a well–to –do yeoman farmer from Chilwell Farm in Cumnor, the year following his arrival in Oxford, on 21 February 1829 at

29

All Saints Church in Oxford. The banns read show that both were by that time living in the city of Oxford. A newspaper advertisement from 1862 records Adin's thanks to his clients for the business they had provided to his tailor's establishment at University House, 136, High Street, Oxford, for "the last 34 years". This placed the start of the business at around 1828, when Adin was 25.

Eliza Williams (nee Bolton)'s father, William, was an early investor in the newly developed Summertown (or as it was originally known "Somers Town"), which was created as a separate Georgian village to the North of Oxford. The fascinating "Origins, History and Description of Summertown in 1832" – a slightly gossipy round –up of the locals and their residences put together by the rector John Badcock in the 1830s – gives a vivid description of who lived where and what they were like. From this account, it can be learned that by 1932 William Bolton had invested in two plots of land in the new development. He owned *"two poor cottages under one roof"*, which he acquired through purchase, and these houses were at the Church Street (now Rogers Street) end of George Street (now Middle Way). He built in 1824 a

> *"comfortable stone –faced house with sash windows and oak coloured door shutters ... [with] a yard [behind] and outbuildings"*.

This house was originally lived in by Mr Bolton's older daughter Mary Ann (known as Ann), who married a relative, Jason Bolton, a butcher. By 1832 the newlyweds had vacated the property, and it was inhabited by the Coulson siblings. By 1841 the Williams family had moved into this property, and Adin was the head of the household with his elderly in –laws also in residence. Father –in –law was to die shortly after this at his Chilwell Farm, and Adin's wife Eliza seems after his death to have moved in with her daughter Martha Wallis and her new husband Harry Neville Prior, initially in nearby Farringdon, and latterly to Sunbury Lodge in Oxford, also a property of the Priors. As a result, from the 1840s, Adin became the owner of Church House – whether, by gift or purchase, it is hard to tell.

The location of this property was the corner of Middle Way and Rogers Street, now the location of the far from lovely North Oxford Conservative Club. In William Bolton's will, the Church House property does not seem to be included in the various bequests, although some Summertown properties are and are referred to as

> "*my freehold messuage or tenement hereditaments and premises together with the cottages adjoining the same with their appurtenances situate and being in Summertown*"

– this is more suggestive of the "*two poor cottages under one roof*" plot of land, as opposed to the stone-built house that Adin was to occupy until shortly before his death.

I wonder about the life that Eliza Williams lived. As suggested below, Adin may not have been the easiest of men to live with. Driven and ubiquitous in Oxford local politics, he may have spent more time away from the family than with it. Her children seem to have left home relatively quickly except for those plagued with issues, and her son George was perhaps to be the cause of a

31

family rift. Of her own family, almost all her siblings emigrated to Wisconsin. She seems to have found comfort in the home of her youngest daughter and her charismatic if financially foolish husband, my great grandfather.

Whether Adin actually himself worked as a mercer or simply directed the business is unclear, but as the family seemed initially to have lived over the shop, it looks likely that he was hands –on. Certainly, in his death certificate, his son Daniel described him simply as *"formerly a tailor"*. He had wide –ranging interests. He was a trustee in bankruptcy for failed concerns, warden of the Mercers and Grocers company and Guardian of the poor. He was also a Street Commissioner. He was first returned as a Guardian of All Saints parish in 1831 when he was only 28. He was also active in politics and held firm liberal beliefs. Family papers suggest that he was Gladstone's political agent when Gladstone was MP for Oxford, and local newspaper reports show that he also supported the local MP Mr Harcourt in 1837, running his campaign from his offices in the High Street. He was extremely active in local affairs, including sitting on the board for the new railway, and as his will demonstrates, he was also an enthusiastic investor in local real estate – although not always as careful with his building or maintenance schemes as he should have been.[10]

University House at 136, High Street was occupied by the family as a family home during at least the early years of

---

[10] For example, in addition to fines and litigation, in 1845 his development at Folly Bridge in St Aldates – a four –storey brick house – collapsed inwards; it was described disparagingly as a "gingerbread building".

the marriage – certainly until at least 1833 but no later than 1841. The house itself seems subsequent to have been redeveloped in the twentieth century, but whilst occupied by the Adin Williams family, it was already a Georgian redevelopment of an earlier house.

On 4th November 1837, *Jackson's Oxford Journal* advertised a forthcoming sale of

> "*a very desirable dwelling house, with an excellent front Shop, situate in the High – street, Oxford, in the occupation of Mr Adin Williams, mercer, &c*",

Adin having been in occupation by this time for around nine years. It is not clear why the house was for sale nor indeed whether Adin then purchased it (perhaps having rented it previously) as he continued to maintain premises there until his death in 1876 and bequeathed the freehold of the property by his will.

In 1851 part of the house was occupied by Adin Williams junior, Adin's son and Ivy's uncle. He was an assistant mercer, described as the head of the household despite being only 16; a 25 –year –old assistant and a servant lived with him. The second part of this house was occupied by Miss Frances Green (57), and the third by Miss Catherine Parker (62) and her servant. Adin senior, by then, lived with the rest of his family in Summertown at Church House. This property (which, as described above, may have come to him from his father –in – law) was part of the very recent development of the area now known as Summertown. Summer Town (originally Somers Town) was an area of about 62 acres between two turnpikes – Banbury and Woodstock roads – which from about 1830 began to be developed as a new village. Church Street (subsequently Rogers Street) ran parallel to and between both turnpikes. The area attracted a diverse population of artisans and businessmen, old and young. Church House no longer exists but seems to have been on a plot of land as a detached dwelling on the corner of what is now Middle Way (and was then George Street) and Church Street, presumably close to (probably the opposite) the Church that was at the time there. 136, High Street remained a prestigious and central location for business, but with a growing family, Adin may well have sought a more tranquil residence away from the workplace and from cholera that infected much of Oxford in the 1840s due to poor drainage and sewerage provisions.

In 1861 Adin Williams junior (26) and his two female cousins were at home with the servants on Census night at 136, High Street. Adin senior remained at Church House until shortly before his death. In the 1861 Census, the address is given as George Street, but in all likelihood the house was on a corner plot which bordered both roads, and the family had not moved.

Adin Williams senior died at 136, High Street house on 11 October 1876. He moved from Church House in Summertown at some time prior to his death, although his will still describes Church House as his residence. His ailing son Daniel was the informant on his death certificate, which gives the cause of death as *"two days apoplexy"*. That probably means that he had a stroke or aneurism. The occupation is given not as political agent or *"gentleman"* as was customary and as adopted by other members of the family, but *"formerly a tailor"*, which looks almost deliberately dismissive. Whilst Adin had struck out from his family home and resettled his own young family in Oxford, his final resting place was at Cote in the graveyard at the Congregational Chapel; neither his wife nor any of his offspring are buried there.

Adin's executors wasted no time in disposing of his property, and an auction of his surplus stock and furniture to be held on the premises was advertised in *Jackson's Oxford Journal* of 18 November 1876:

"136 HIGH STREET, OXFORD,
To Clothiers, Mercers, Furniture
Dealers, and Householders.

Important sale of SURPLUS STOCK – IN –TRADE, consisting of 19 yards of black Angola, 108 yards fancy ditto and Tweeds, 20 short lengths doeskin Angolas, 30 fancy waistcoat pieces, 63 yards shirting, 24 white and coloured shirts, mackintoshes, scarlet jerseys, 74 hats and caps, 55 dozen linen collars, gloves, hat bands, and studs, 300 scarves, ties and bows, University gowns and hoods, morning cloaks, quantity of ready –made clothing, &c.

The HOUSEHOLD FURNITURE comprises mahogany dining and telescope tables, excellent mahogany sideboards, very handsome walnut dwarf bookcase, mahogany ditto, walnut settees in green damask, handmade mahogany chiffonière bookcase, ditto easy chairs in marone, reps, and leather, mahogany cornice poles, crimson and damask curtains, iron French, half –tester, and other bedsteads, palliasses, wool and flock mattresses, bolsters and pillows, blankets, feather beds, chests of drawers in mahogany, walnut, and oak, dressing tables, Cyclopean glasses, Turkey, Kidderminster, and other carpets and rugs (nearly new), kitchen utensils, and other miscellaneous effects."

Nonetheless, the family maintained a commercial interest in the property until at least 1880. Records show that the occupiers of the site at 136, High Street between 1830 and 1910 were:

Downstairs (i.e. shop) – 1830 –1876 Adin Williams Tailor and Mercer – (personally until 1861); thereafter, Hugh James Allen Tailor and robe maker Hugh Allen moved to (or expanded into) 138, High Street in 1913.

Upstairs – offices – 1848 TB Montrie, professor of dancing; 1866 Adin Williams' son George St Swithin Williams, solicitor (1866) and Frederick Codd, architect.[11]

1872 Oxon & Berks Bank (a further business of George St. Swithin Williams).

1880 St. Swithin Williams, solicitor.

1882 –1889 W Geekie.

1894 –1899 A Ballard, solicitor.

1900 –1901 Stephen Salter, architect.

During his life, Adin acquired considerable real estate in Oxford, either by direct purchase or through the practice – developed by his son – of purchasing ground rents. He also diversified from his business as a mercer not only into real estate (where he was not always successful in his building enterprises[12]) and established in his business premises an agency for Star Fire and Life Assurance.

As foreshadowed above, family opinion is that life in Adin's household may not have been completely happy. At various times the family seems to have been split: for example, Adin junior seems to have remained in 136, High Street whilst his father moved to Summertown; this included sharing quarters with their relatives from Shifford (adjacent to Cote), the Wallis family, as was recorded in the 1861 Census referred to above. Adin was

---

[11] Codd was to be one of the architects of the newly formed King Edward Street, to which George St Swithin Williams moved upon his family's return to Oxford.

[12] See previous reference to his "gingerbread" building.

37

a busy man. As summarised above, records suggest that he was a political agent for Gladstone, who was MP for Oxford University from 1847 and prior to that from 1837 for Mr G Harcourt as well as running the mercer's shop at 136, High Street (bear in mind the reference above to the corruption of Oxford politics). Immediately after Adin acquired his property in 1837, he seems to have designated it as the headquarters for Mr Harcourt (*Oxford Journal* 29 July 1837), who was subsequently re –elected MP. Ironically for the Liberal Adin, Harcourt subsequently became a Tory.

Adin found himself at odds with local authority from time to time, although he was also a diligent member of the community. He became a Guardian of the poor for All Saints in 1831 (aged 28), was a warden of the Mercers and Grocers company in 1843, and a trustee in bankruptcy. In 1844 he was involved in the route of the railway line proposed for Oxford, and the following year was a provincial committee member for the Oxford and Salisbury direct railway line. His involvement with Gladstone seems to have stemmed from about 1846.

He was active in fundraising for the church, lending his garden for a tea party for the Congregational Church in 1853. Between 1856 and 1863, at least he was a Street Commissioner for road works, gas lighting and water works in Oxford and acted as chair. His interests were fairly wide –ranging; for example, in 1846, he offered a rick of hay for sale in nearby Woolton, and in 1865 he was petitioning against the evils of the liquor trade. He made donations to a children's ward for a clock and statues.

In 1864 he was involved in an insurrection in Summertown for not paying his church rates (on a matter of principle), and in 1870 was fined for allowing a chimney fire at 136 High Street. The same year he objected to the development of a new police court, which he asserted threatened his right to light.

In 1865 he was a committee member for promoting three Liberal candidates: Philip Pleydell Bouverie, John Walker and George G Craven. He sued for unpaid rent unsuccessfully in 1867 and brought another suit in 1874 on behalf of his son Horace, which again failed. In 1875 he was summoned for nuisance.

Adin was 28 when his eldest daughter Eliza Ruth was born and 47 when his youngest, Martha Wallis, arrived. Of his eight children born between 1831 and 1850, the three girls married relatively early (Eliza Ruth in 1855, aged 24, Mary Abigail in 1865, aged 21, and Martha Wallis in 1870, aged 20). Adin seems to have approved of all their husbands, naming two of them executors, the third being a prominent missionary who spent much of his time overseas. Tellingly the one solicitor in the family, Ivy's father, George St. Swithin, was not named as executor. An explanation for this is considered later.

The sons all presented their own problems. George, the eldest and Ivy's father, whom we shall meet later, qualified as a solicitor in 1854. He does not seem to have attended university. His business affairs were entrepreneurial, and he was a regular correspondent with newspaper editors on issues of the day, especially tax. Born plain George, on entering the business, he changed his name, adding "St. Swithin" to distinguish himself from the many other George Williams in the business world. The story of his marriage and the birth of his two children is told in more detail hereafter. He was a solicitor, banker and gentleman, a man of strong personality who at one time refused to pay his income tax because of his disappointment with the way in which it was being used by the country. He can be seen as a radical, a man of high energy and great passions. He had a close and supportive relationship with Ivy. He seems to have been the dominant personality in the household. He remained a bachelor until he was in his late thirties, living at home with his opinionated father before apparently breaking away and setting up his own business, working more often with his wife's family than his own.

George's brother Adin (junior), born in 1835, seems to have been dogged by mental health issues and significant depression all his life and to have spent time in a mental institution. He worked for his father as an assistant mercer at one stage. Although he married, he does not seem to have had children and committed suicide by drowning, leaving a poignant note exonerating all his family who had all tried and failed to help him. In his later years, he was apparently supported by George, being unable to work, although the terms of Adin's will do make provision for him, so possibly the challenge to the will may have held that up.

Daniel, born in 1837, was an invalid all his life and carefully provided for by Adin. He died in the Homeopathic Hospital, Bath, in 1885. His executor was his brother Henry Bulteel who only acted some five years later at a time when probate was regularly obtained within months of death.

Henry Bulteel seems to have spent some time abroad and returned to marry Elizabeth Miller in the Kensington district at the end of 1881. From his work as executor for his brother Daniel in around 1890, he was described as an upholsterer of 105, Clarendon Road, Notting Hill, and when he died in 1894, aged 48, he was living with his wife at 61, Portland Road, West Brighton where he kept a lodging house. He had three children, Ernest, Arthur and Henry. Arthur moved to Leatherhead, and Percy Prior (his cousin and Ivy's solicitor) corresponded with him in 1923 about his father's estate. Percy also wrote to Henry (who had moved to Ontario) and to Ernest (who had moved to Toronto, although there are also links with Brighton), stating that he and Harry Neville Prior, as executors of Adin Williams' will, would be paying out the proceeds from the sale of cottages which had been invested. Henry Bulteel was presumably named for the popular Oxford radical preacher Henry Bulteel of the day. There is a little early record of him except for a rare mention of a drunk and disorderly event in Newbury in 1874, Henry being described as a *"jobbing carpenter"*; whether this is a different Henry Bulteel or an early act of rebellion, given the teetotal household kept by Adin senior, is uncertain.

John Horace (sometimes Horatio) seems to have been the black sheep of the family or simply deeply unhappy with his life in England. He married young Sarah Ann and had two daughters, Lilian Maria, born in 1872 and Sarah Elizabeth, born in 1874. By the time Lilian married in 1889, she had described her father as dead (and formerly a tailor) when in reality, he had emigrated to Ontario, where he remained all his life. Ivy took pity on him in the 1920s and sent him money. He died at Simcoe in Ontario, aged 84, in 1930.

Martha Wallis married Harry Neville Prior, a happy and popular man who seems to have made and lost a fortune – they had six children.

It is against this background of a family with strong personalities and many frailties that the union of Ivy's parents might be set.

Chapter 3
Early years

The union of George St. Swithin Williams and Emma Ewers appears controversial.

On the face of it, the facts are these.

In 1871 George St. Swithin and two of his brothers, Daniel and John Horace, were living with their parents, Adin and Eliza Williams, in Church House, Church Street, Summertown, Oxford. John Horace, described as a master tailor and mercer, was about to marry Sarah Ann Bateman, and younger sister Martha Wallis had the previous year married Harry Neville Prior. George had a solicitors' office over his father's upholstery shop at 136, High Street, Oxford. George was 38. George had, therefore, an extremely close relationship of necessity with his father, with whom he both lived and worked.

George was already a hustler. He established his first "bank" (a lending organisation) in 1854, the year he qualified as a solicitor. In 1857 he acted in a high –profile case for an unseated council member, and in 1861 was involved as a lawyer in several Oxford bankruptcy cases as a solicitor advocate. The same year he was offering services as the Oxford office of Anglo –Saxon Investment Association of London, New York, Melbourne and Sydney as an investment vehicle and lender – also from

136, High Street. In 1862 he advertised his business of money lending and debt collecting from 136, High Street, although in 1863, he also used an address at 7, St Aldates and was offering a discounting service for trade bills. He offered loans from £5 to £300 secured. He was vocal in his views on politics, writing to the newspapers in 1865 with his opinion on the malt tax; in 1867, he wrote a long anti –invasion letter. By 1869 he was able to offer loans for as much as £1,000. He announced his liberal sympathies in a letter about the Oxford Republican Society, speaking about "real" liberalism.

As surmised above, the family home may not have been the easiest place to live. George's father, Adin, was known for his confrontational style of doing business and insistence on his rights, his strong religious views and his busy life as a member of the Oxford political society. His three daughters had all left home fairly early (all had married by 1870 in their early twenties), as had two other sons, leaving the three boys. Whilst George was undoubtedly an able businessman with a fine intellect, his brothers were less fortunate. Of Adin junior and his issues, we have already heard. Daniel, the next born, was one of the three who remained at the family home in 1871. He suffered from a long –term illness that required constant nursing and died in 1885. Still at home but shortly to wed was John Horatio Williams. After a disastrous married life, John Horatio was to abandon his family and emigrate to Canada, where his wife and daughters (and in all probability, his immediate family) regarded him as dead.

In 1871, aged seventeen, Emma Ewers was the household's domestic servant. Emma was the daughter of the late Harriett Ewers (nee Hawkins), the former servant to the family.

In 1875 Emma registered the birth of George's son, Winter Williams, in Ryde, Isle of Wight, correcting her name from Ewers to Williams in the registration form. There is no sign of any marriage certificate. The couple did not return to Oxford until after the birth of Ivy in 1877 in Newton Abbot after the death of Adin Williams in 1876.

Plausibly the relationship between Emma and George did not meet with the approval of Adin senior and led to an estrangement. Adin did not appoint George – his solicitor son – as an executor in his will, although he did make provision for him. Confusingly Ivy refers affectionately to her grandfather, whom she never met, in her speeches, suggesting that her father similarly had a good relationship in spite of what looks like a period of banishment to the south coast.

However, put in the greater context, what actually arose may be something quite different and more symptomatic of a caring and open –minded family – suggesting that Ivy was born into a loving and close family.[13]

---

[13] That Ivy enjoyed a warm and caring home life whilst living with her parents is borne out by a speech that she made in September 1905 about what makes a happy home (drawing parallels with what makes a happy church). She referred to cheery, bright and happy homes with a groundwork of love where everyone worked to a common cause as being the best, and further stated that the highest kind of home welcomed guests warmly. There seems little doubt that she was drawing on her own memories in this speech.

In 1851 the Williams family employed as house maid Harriet Hawkins, then aged 26 when the young George was 17 and a solicitor's clerk (perhaps surprisingly, there is no indication that George attended university). Harriett, who was illiterate, married a local mason and general labourer, Joseph Ewers, shortly after. Joseph, sometimes also described as a servant, lived next door but one. George qualified as a solicitor in 1854, shortly before Harriet Hawkins – then Ewers – gave birth to Emma. Harriet had five children by 1866: Emma (the oldest), Charles, born in 1857; Rosa, born in 1860, Thomas Edward, born in 1863; and Ernest, born in 1866. The Ewers family lived in Summertown, not far from the Williams.

A double tragedy struck the Ewers family in 1868. On 24 February, Harriett Ewers died a day after giving birth to a daughter, also christened Harriett privately on the same day – hopefully, while her mother still lived. Harriett senior died from loss of blood and exhaustion from the birth; she was buried on 28 March *"on coroners orders"* (suggesting an inquest was held into the cause of death), aged 41. Emma was then aged 13, Charles 11, Rosa 8, Thomas 5, and Ernest 2. Baby Harriett died two weeks after her mother and was buried in the same grave.

The impact of Harriett senior's death on this young family is hard to imagine. Not only had they lost a mother, but they also had to endure the coroner's enquiry and the loss of their tiny sister. It is very likely that no immediate steps were taken to split the family up: a year later, in 1869, Joseph had the 12 –year –old Charles with him during his work as a carrier. But the family was around; the

Carpenters (described as Joseph's brothers) lived on the same and adjacent roads, and there was an uncle in Cowley.

But worse was to follow ... Within a year, Joseph Ewers – who seems to have taken work as a carrier – was killed.

On 19 May 1869, a year after his wife's death, Joseph took a party of eight or nine people from Summertown in his horse –drawn coal van to the Eynsham Athletic Sports. In the evening, on the way back, they called in at the Red Lion at Cassington. A dispute arose with a man called John Timms. As Joseph was readying his horse for the return journey, he was struck four times by Timms with a hatchet. His young son was with him at the time and will have witnessed it all. Joseph's friends took him in his own cart to the Radcliffe infirmary, but he discharged himself prematurely on 2 June, prior to his wounds healing. He was re –admitted on 12 July, having suffered inflammation of the brain and convulsions, and died the following day, aged 37.

After an inquest on 14 July, Joseph was buried in Summertown on 16 July 1868. The verdict at the Spring Assizes of 3 March 1870 was one of manslaughter reduced from murder on the basis that Joseph should not have discharged himself from the hospital. He was also found to have kidney disease, which contributed to his death. Timms was sentenced to 18 months in prison. Whilst today these events seem cataclysmic, in the context of the day, they were far from unusual. Burial records for the cemetery where the two Harrietts were interred show that of the 15 entries on the same page, several were for children under the age of 5. Of the cases tried by the Oxford Assizes at the same time as the charge against Timms, there was a further charge of murder, several rape cases including attempted rape of a child under 10, several cases of arson and one of bestiality!

The children were orphaned. There seems to have been a swift rescue by friends and family, as in the 1871 Census, Charles and Ernest were billeted with their uncle Israel Carpenter, a milkman, in George Street.

Rosa was housed with her uncle Jonathan, a coal porter and local preacher, in Cowley. Thomas was initially boarded at Witney, and he surfaced next as a labourer in Mitcham, Surrey, in 1881. Emma, the oldest, was taken into employment as a servant by the Williams family. When this happened is not known; nor can we ascertain whether she did this to help support the family after her mother's death or only after her father died.

In any event, at some time between early 1871 and 1875, Emma and George forged a relationship that was to endure until George's death in 1904.

Their first child, Winter (a family name), was born on 17 September 1875 at Elmfield, Ryde, Isle of Wight. Why he was born there is a matter of speculation: the most likely reason is that George had felt obliged to take his young wife away from Oxford, perhaps given the disapproval of his father. In the absence of a marriage certificate, the couple may even have eloped, Emma being a minor at the time; they may possibly have married very privately or even in Scotland.

At around this time, George seems to have maintained offices in London – for example, he faced suit in 1875 for the performance of an agreement to transfer a mortgage over reversionary interest to widow Dwell. In the process documents his address is given as "Rolls Court" London; he describes himself in the years that he did not live in Oxford as a "gentleman", for example, in the birth certificates of his children. By this time, George had built up something of a nest egg for himself and had, of course, run his own business (albeit from his father's premises), so he was quite likely to have been able to fund his "gap year(s)". Winter's birth certificate was signed by his mother, who started to sign in her maiden name but corrected it to Williams (suggesting perhaps either a recent marriage or possibly no marriage at all). His father's name is given (as it was for all "non –business" matters) as simply George Williams. It took 38 days for the registration to be completed, which is a surprising length of time in comparison with other births registered by the family at the time. There may have been a number of reasons for this – ill health of child or mother, or absence perhaps of a father; but perhaps the most likely is the recently introduced provisions of the Births and Deaths Act 1874, which made registration compulsory from 1875 (prior to that time the onus was on local registrars to ascertain births, marriages and deaths, which led to a high percentage of births being unregistered). The 1874 Act switched the onus onto the parents to volunteer the relevant details and imposed penalties for failure to do so. The current 42 –day requirement was introduced in 1875 and has remained unchanged.

Ivy was born in Newton Abbot on 7 September 1877 in Devon Square, a gracious Regency Square in the town centre. Her mother once again registered the birth, and her father is simply named "George Williams, Gentleman". It took 39 days for Emma to register the birth. So far as I am aware, there had been no other Ivy in either family, in a time when families (in particular the Williams) regularly honoured family names. Why the family had moved to Newton Abbot from Ryde (and whether they had lived anywhere else in the interim) is unknown. Ivy's grandfather had died in 1876, the year before her arrival, and probably never knew that she was on the way. In due course, the family returned to Oxford.

After Adin's death in 1876, there appears to have been some family fallout over the provisions of his will. We know this, as in his own will George St. Swithin Williams refers to that litigation and to the financial and emotional cost of it to the family; he stipulated that if there was a challenge to his own will, any bequests to the challenger should stand void. Whilst it is now impossible to track down details of the litigation about Adin's will, the comment about the voiding of the bequest by George suggests that it was a beneficiary who made the intervention.

The will had originally identified three executors, one of whom declined to take up the position, and it may well have been that executor – William Baker, George's brother –in –law – who challenged Adin's will. He seems, on balance, the most likely objector. Adin's will provided little of real value to certain of his children apart from life interests. This may be because he had already provided for them in his lifetime (although there is evidence to the contrary, for example, the troubled Adin Williams junior, who suffered from what seems to have been a bipolar condition and depression and was supported once he found himself unable to work by his brother George, not by his father).

Adin's will provided that it be executed by two of his sons –in –law: Harry Neville Prior (then an upholsterer of nearby Farringdon) and William Baker (also a cabinet maker and upholsterer of Oxford, with whom Prior was to enter a probably disastrous business partnership in due course), together with his friend John Lindsey, a butcher and neighbour from Summertown. An obvious omission as executor was George, the family solicitor. In the event Baker declined, Adin's widow Eliza assumed the role of the third executor. Eliza was close to Prior and lived with him after her husband's death.

The will gave Adin's wife Eliza the household effects from Church House in Summertown and use of the house for her life (subject to a proviso that she allows her daughter Mary Abigail and family to reside there with her if they so wished). Adin's separation from his family in Cote seems to have been complete, as, through his will, he left only bequests to his immediate family in Oxford.[14]

The will gave personal gifts of the family bible to the Bakers; the second bible to son Daniel; a watch to son Henry Bulteel; the second family watch to Adin; to John Horace the Bradley sermons; to Mary Abigail Cousins, his second daughter, his piano. Nothing personal for his youngest daughter (wife of Harry Neville Prior), son John nor to George St. Swithin.

---

[14] In spite of which alone of the Oxford family, Adin was buried in Cote.

51

Of his debts and monies owed to him on mortgages, these were to be collected in. From this, it is likely that Adin had participated in – may even have originated – the lending business assumed by George (and indeed, to a lesser extent by the various nephews and nieces, including Ivy in due course). He excluded from collection a loan made to Harry Neville, which was effectively assigned to his wife Martha, who was to receive the interest from it. This was a slightly unusual arrangement within a family whereby the wife was entitled to monies from the husband – and may have indicated a concern by Adin as to the financial prudence of her husband and the need for Martha to have her own income. Daniel, the invalid, was given the sum of £300 (about £12,000 today).

Of Adin's large portfolio of Oxford real estate, he provided as follows:

Church House to his wife for life (and available to Mary Abigail) and thereafter to Mary Abigail. It is perhaps of interest that Mary Abigail and her family retained a home at Chalfont Road in Oxford at all times but that they did acquire title to Church House with the intention (not recognised at least for some of the time) of leasing it out. Records show the house to have been in poor repair when it was sold to a neighbour in 1895, having fallen into the estate of William Cousins through the death of his wife, Mary Abigail. It was sold for a net £585 –12 –8d to the Rev Henry Anstey. It may be because of the state of repair that the house was subsequently demolished.

To his wife, income from 136, High Street, and 4 properties in Blenheim Place and Plantation Road – with a request that she should apply the income to the education of his grandchildren and that in due course these be sold and added to the grandchildren's fund.

Martha, his youngest daughter, was to get a second property in Summertown, then occupied by Jon Busby and part of the orchard from Church House (the Busby property stood almost opposite Church House); and the debt owed by her husband, Harry Neville.

George was to get a parcel of land to situate at the west end of Grove Street in Summertown *"now in my own occupation"* (this is not, I think to be confused with Church House, which had been bequeathed to Adin's wife and then to Mary Abigail, but simply implied that the property was not tenanted). Grove Street ran parallel to Church Street, so it seems Adin had invested quite widely in his immediate neighbourhood.

He also held property and land in Speedwell Street in Oxford, and income from that was to be used to educate his son John's daughters – John having it seems abandoned the family. They were to receive the properties absolutely upon reaching the age of 24.

Other land Adin held in St Aldates and in Speedwell Street was to be held on trust for Adin junior and his wife. On their death, it was to be sold, and the proceeds paid to his grandchildren.

The land he held in Thames Street and in Wellington Street in Jericho was to be held in trust for his son Henry Buteel and thereafter for his lawful children (of whom in the event there were three) – or if none, to the grandchildren at large.

Property at 9, Thames Street was to be held in trust for Daniel for life and thereafter to go to the general fund for the grandchildren.

In short, apart from personal gifts of mainly sentimental value, Adin only gave the property to his children, Martha Wallis, Mary Abigail and George. All other property was given to various of his children for a life interest only and thereafter to be divided between his grandchildren. His eldest daughter Eliza and her husband William Baker got nothing of significant value except that their children participated in the general fund for the grandchildren. At the time, Eliza was 45, and the couple had an adopted daughter born in 1858; there were subsequently further children, William and Hilda, born in 1872 and 1874, respectively when Eliza was in her forties and after she had been married for 23 years. There is some family feeling that William may not have been the father.

Why Adin chose to exclude them but still expected William to act as executor is hard to understand. Perhaps he thought them sufficiently wealthy – William Baker had, after all, been responsible for substantial buildings in the centre of Oxford, one of which still bears his name (on which basis it is hard to see why Adin had given property to George, who seems to have been similarly well endowed). Perhaps he didn't like them. Their family arrangements were not orthodox. Their adopted daughter Constance Jeffries is subsequently referred to as a servant or domestic help in the house; their two children came along very late in the marriage and perhaps controversially. By 1891 Eliza was ailing and taking the waters in Matlock: she died in 1901. Whatever the reason, it is very likely that Adin seriously miscalculated the impact of this omission and that it started inter –family litigation, which seems to have stung and was still a source of unhappiness when George St. Swithin died in 1904. Certainly, in terms of family relations, Ivy seems to have had almost no contact with the Bakers and to have been closest to the Cousins and Priors. It very much looks as if the Priors' financial failures were in part caused by the partnership with the Bakers (and possibly a lack of financial prudence by Harry Neville).

The other candidate for a challenge to the will is Adin's son John. He was also not mentioned in the will, although his children were given a specific bequest as well as participation in the general grandchildren's fund. Whilst it is fairly clear that John was the black sheep of the family and deserted his responsibilities, it seems similarly unlikely that he would have challenged the will: by the time of Adin's death, he had almost certainly emigrated to Canada, and his wife appears to have been given a payoff (she is described as an annuitant in the 1881 Census and had family locally who worked as domestic servants with whom her children seem to have stayed).

Because of the life interests created, the will would take in excess of 45 years to be administered, with life interests and final accounts still being handled by Percy Prior (executor Harry Neville's solicitor son) in the 1920s.

The grandchildren's fund was comprised of land in which Adin's wife Eliza held an interest in Blenheim Place and Plantation road, which fell into the trust with her death in 1901; it was supplemented in 1908 with the land left to Adin junior's wife on trust in St Aldates and Speedwell street; in 1885 Daniel had died leaving 9, Thames street to create the initial fund.

Who were the grandchildren who benefitted from this fund?

Adin's will was very specific that female grandchildren were to take in their own right. All were to inherit absolutely on obtaining 24 years of age, the girls earlier if they married earlier. Anyone who died before attaining 24 was to take per stirpes – which in context seems to mean that their share would revert to any siblings. The Bakers had three children if the adopted Constance Jeffries was included; George was to have two, of whom one was living at the time of Adin's will. Adin junior and Daniel had none. Mary Abigail had six who survived to adulthood, and all of whom were alive at the time Adin made his will. Henry Bulteel had three children; John had two who were treated as special cases by Adin, perhaps reflecting his disapproval of their father, who himself got nothing under the will. Martha had at the time of the will one child but would go on to have six. The youngest grandchild was born in 1895, meaning that the fund technically remained open until at the earliest 1929 before the youngest could take his share.

On the whole, the will reflects a possible tendency by Adin to try to control things even after his death. The format was not particularly unusual in that it was common to create life interests for wives and dependants, but the selection of specific properties for each branch of the family and the insistence on the importance of education may have rankled his adult children, who had by then their own plans and ambitions. The value of the estate was put in 1875 at less than £6,000 (about £750,000 today). To us, that looks like a very small return on some prime real estate in central Oxford, and if liquidated to that equivalent sum, left relatively little for distribution between the 22 grandchildren unless there was some very successful investment in the intervening period or the price of real estate rose significantly prior to the land falling into the trust from time to time (which it probably did). In any event, although a pleasant distribution and of huge assistance for the education of the children, the sum, in the end, would not have made a significant difference to the lives of the grandchildren. When for example, Harry Neville Prior fell on hard times, his youngest two sons had to be removed from education at Magdalen College School.

That Ivy was able to complete a thorough home education and in her time be a major philanthropist in her hometown, as well as being a benefactor both to the university and her community, speaks more to her father's enterprising nature than to any significant monetary inheritance from her grandfather. From him, however, she derived a passion for politics, a sense of civic and family responsibility and strongly held religious beliefs.

After Adin's death, George St. Swithin returned to Oxford and, in due course, took up residence in 12, King Edward Street, which was remodelled for him prior to his return. It was a time of change in the world and not just in Oxford. In 1876 in the United States, the Battle of Little Bighorn (Custer's Last stand) took place with heavy loss by the US cavalry; the telephone was invented that same year. Bicycle use had become common in England by the

1870s: Winter Williams was to be a keen cyclist and member of the cycling club at Oxford, and Ivy's cousin Sydney ran a bicycle shop and later built motor cars, which started to appear in the streets of Oxford in around 1915. Ivy herself kept a horse and rode side –saddle or drove a trap until February 1909, when ill health obliged her to sell horse and equipment *"owing to the illness of owner and physician's advice"*. She held a driving license for much of her life.

The time of George's permanent removal to King Edward Street would be around 1884 – certainly, until 1883 the surgeon Robert Thomas Jenkins (who attended Adin on his death bed) had been in residence at 12, King Edward Street. The precise dating of the arrival of the family is difficult to pin down. It is consistent with George's preferences that he chose a new build as his family home, as he would subsequently when he purchased Sunnyside in Cowley.

King Edward Street was a road of new buildings created in 1872/73 by Oriel College, which demolished two houses to join the High Street to Oriel Square. Pevsner was not impressed by the architecture, describing the street as *"a street of any old –town centre. Just rows of four –storey houses, all drab except no 8 the far corner – house, which is gothic of yellow brick and stone"*. That said, the work of the architect Codd who designed the houses to the west of the street, is well regarded. Codd had shared premises with the Williams whilst at 136, High Street, so it is possible that he kept in touch and introduced George to the chance of leasing premises in the road from Oriel College, which retains title to the entire street to this day.

Throughout his time away from Oxford George continued to be recorded as keeping premises in 89, Chancery Lane, although this seems to be more in the nature of a lawyers' chambers than anything else – a post restante, if you will. His court cases in Oxford seem to have been suspended between 1872 and 1880, suggesting he was not in Oxford for much of that time. In 1880 Jacksons records his return to Oxford, where he is still shown as keeping premises upstairs in 136, High Street as a solicitor. The family per se do not appear in the 1881 or 1891 Census at all.

George had inherited a house in Summertown in Grove Street from Adin, and it may be that he took up temporary residence therefrom 1880 pending finding a permanent residence for the family. In1882, the local newspaper reported that work was being done at 9, King Edward Street for George. This is the only reference to George having an interest in 9, King Edward Street. That property was shown in the 1881 Census as the "Reform Club", although the Payne family lived at 8 next door and were subsequently recorded as being lodging –house keepers at 10, King Edward Street in the 1891 Census – suggesting perhaps that 8 and 10 were interconnected. Of potential interest is that the "Reform Club" shows an occupant – William Busby and family. William was a 30 –year –old stonemason. Adin had left Busby's house in Summertown to his daughter Martha Prior, and it is a possibility (if this is the same Busby family) that they had been offered alternative accommodation in the Reform Club whilst the property was sold. The Priors never, so far as I can see, lived in Summertown.

12, King Edward Street was occupied in 1881 by the surgeon Robert Thomas Jenkins – he who had signed Adin's death certificate and was still in situ in 1883. The Oxford Building Society collapsed that same year, and George was by then actively seeking business from the bondholders. Where his family lived, however, is unclear. In the 1891 Census, 12, King Edward Street is added as something of an afterthought: it is inserted informally between 11 and 13 as "Bank". No details of occupants are given. It is quite possible that the premises were accordingly lived in by George's family by 1891, with the lower floors being used for business premises. Robert Jenkins is shown to have been widowed in the intervening period and to have moved to 15, King Edward Street (which may have been smaller). 9 and 10 are occupied by the Paynes as lodging –house keepers and by cooks. Ivy's blue plaque at 12, King Edward street gives her address there as being between 1887 and 1904. The 1901 Census shows the family in residence at 12, King Edward Street (and nowhere else).

George seems to have retained the office space at 136, High Street for his solicitors' practice, which is recorded as his place of work in 1866 and again in 1880. From about 1885, all business seems to be being transacted from 12 King Edward Street, which was named Merton House. George seems to have had several businesses. He describes himself as a solicitor and a banker. He had (at least) two financial businesses; he ran the Oxon & Berks Bank initially from 136, High Street and later from 12,

King Edward Street; he also ran a less formal business, "Oxford Financial Services", from the same addresses. The latter was said to have been founded in 1854 when George would have been 21. There was considerable cross –over between the various businesses. His legal practice enabled him to service the bad debts that the Oxford Financial Services business would buy at a discount. He also lent against mortgages of property, which he was able to document himself.

Ivy's records retained at St Anne's College show that she also lived at some time in Highfield House. This was a substantial house constructed by Harry Neville Prior for his young family in Headington. His daughter Cordelia (and possibly his other daughter Gladys) also were Home –Students in their time and were of a similar age to Ivy, so shared accommodation may have been convenient. When Ivy lived there is unclear; this would seem to have been perhaps at a time when she was "between" houses. The college records would only record addresses relevant to the student's time at the university, and Ivy was not to attend Oxford until 1896. The Priors fell on hard times and had to sell Highfield in 1908, narrowing the window of her likely occupation. Subsequently, Ivy was to live at a new house in Cowley called Sunnyside, to occupy premises in Highgate in Nassington Road, and to spend her last years in "Cote" at 30, Staverton Road, North Oxford.

Ivy's mother, Emma Ewers, was of humbler stock. As described above, her own mother had been the illiterate servant of the Williams before marrying local mason/handyman Joseph. Her siblings, however, were able in carving out successful lives for themselves. Any suggestion of enmity between the Williams and Ewers is rebutted by the fact, for example, that young Charles Ewers subsequently became Ivy's lawyer or financial advisor and was at some time clerk to George St. Swithin Williams. His daughter Florence also seems to have been involved in Williams' business affairs.

Ivy's aunts and uncles on her mother's side were supportive in practical terms of her and her chosen career. After moving initially to work as a clerk on the railways in Sheffield, Charles Ewers seems to have married a slightly older widow with a ready –made family – one Elizabeth Jepson Mawson – and then, on his return to Oxford to have been eventually employed by George. Charles seems to have had a similarly entrepreneurial bent to George, initially working out of a house on Hurst Street in Cowley, offering estate agency, drafting and probate services prior to his removal to King Edward Street. Charles Ewers seems to have moved his business into 12, King Edward Street and to have run his own projects from there in about 1906.

The fact that the young Williams family left Oxford to travel to the south coast for a number of years may have been as much to protect the sensitivities of the community (or indeed just for fun) than in evidence of parental disapproval. A more generous and likely interpretation of events is that the family did the right thing in supporting Emma and that theirs was a love match. Indeed, such correspondence as survives shows a deep affection between the couple and a strong bond and mutual admiration between father and daughter.

I have searched in vain for a picture of George St. Swithin. The only tantalising glimpse I may have seen was through an internet search that threw up a collection of Victorian photographs. In (brief) correspondence with the owner, she claimed that one of them showed George. My recollection of the one to which she referred is of a long – nosed, frankly evil –looking man (which may have explained why he married relatively late in life). The correspondence is now lost and is an abiding loss. I also have a series of photos from the family album, some of which are reproduced in this work: many are un –named, and he could easily be amongst them.

Evidence is that the young Williams family was a close – knit and happy place. Education was extremely valued. Hopes were high for both children, who followed similar academic paths, being home-schooled and excelling in local examinations. Their impressive exam results were often published in the local newspaper, and family records include a picture of Fraulien Vallet, who seems to have been a governess to a branch of the family. Ivy's cousins were educated at the local schools; Robin Silvio and Rex Prior were students at Magdalen College school until his father fell on hard times, and their sisters attended Oxford High School.

Chapter 4
A family of mighty women

Various of Ivy's relatives achieved greatness in one sphere or another, but what is perhaps remarkable is the number of women in the family who were trailblazers or simply brilliant. The Cousins family perhaps most typified what seems to have been a strongly developed sense of the need to serve, to reach out to the world and to do so at full power.

Mary Abigail Williams.

Ivy's aunt Mary Abigail Williams had married the Reverent William Cousins in 1865 at the age of 21. William Cousins is known affectionately in the family as *"great uncle Bartholomew"* perhaps for his impressive beard and the great age he was to achieve. William was a fervent Congregationalist and skilled Greek and Hebrew scholar. It was his mission in life to spread the word of God and work for the good of the natives of Madagascar. Much of his life was spent there, as was that of his brother George. Madagascar had had a stormy history of colonisation by the French and then the British, but with

64

the Victorian age, the intentions of those who went there from the London Missionary Society lay less in colonisation and more in redemption. This brought with it issues that troubled various liberals. Robert Louis Stevenson, for example – known to the Williams family and a long –time resident of Samoa – was troubled by the drive of the missionaries to effect change.

Of missionary work, he considered that

> *"there is some good work to be done in the long run … [but] forget wholly and forever all small pruderies and remember that you cannot change ancestral feelings of right and wrong without what is practically soul –murder. Remember that all you can do is to civilise a man in the line of his own civilisation such as it is".*

This advice was not wasted on the Cousins family. William was entrusted with finalising the translation of the bible into the local Malagasy, but his approach as chairman of a committee that met over a significant period of time in Madagascar was to include the local people in the process in order to ensure that the translation was not only accurate and meaningful but also relevant to them.

William seems to have commanded a decent house in Madagascar, but the arrival of his young bride at their destination after a long and, in part, very basic voyage can only be imagined. Mary Abigail is shown as a slender and neat young person and features in many of the family photos. She was clearly a darling of the family, being left specific gifts by her father in his will and mentioned in various other documents. She left a comfortable home in

Oxford from which it is unlikely that she travelled much prior to her marriage to make the journey to Madagascar and was to spend the greater part of the rest of her life there. As a missionary wife, she would have been expected to teach and assist with the running of the missionary, primarily staffed by men. In Antananarivo, she gave birth to seven children, the first of whom lived less than a year.

The work of the missionaries in Madagascar and the perils they faced are well documented. The attitude of the local queen towards them was ambivalent. At times it became hostile, and "converts" from time to time faced serious repercussions. This may explain why William brought to Oxford local boys and a local woman: perhaps to save them from persecution or else to further their education. Whatever the reason, according to my grandfather, it was "*not a success*".

Records show that George Cousins was accompanied by his wife in his time in Madagascar, but there is scant mention of Mary Abigail, whose health seems to have suffered eventually and who had returned to Oxford by 1891. There is little doubt that the couple set out for Madagascar almost as soon as they were married and a charming photo of the family taken around 1875 shows a relaxed and comfortable gathering, the parents dressed in full Victorian England clothing with their sons asserting their personalities in more novel outfits.

I list Mary Abigail as an influence on Ivy even though her departure for Madagascar predated Ivy's birth, and she died whilst Ivy was still relatively young. The family kept in contact through letter –writing and visits when on leave, and without doubt, the bravery and commitment of Abigail Mary and her willingness to step into the unknown will have been a significant influence on Ivy.

Of more immediate influence is perhaps the work of two of Ivy's Cousins cousins, with whom she maintained a regular correspondence and met whenever the opportunity presented itself.

Ethel Constance Cousins.

Ethel (known as Constance) was Ivy's first cousin – daughter of Mary Abigail Williams and the missionary William Edward Cousins. Constance was their youngest child, born five years after Ivy and was only nine years old when her mother died. Her father continued his mission in Madagascar, where she was born, but she was educated in England in a school for the children of missionaries in Walthamstow Hall.[15]

Constance studied in Oxford between 1900 and 1904, and there are records of her visits to the Williams, where for example, on 10 March 1891, she attended a baptism with Ada Cousins (her sister born in Madagascar in 1874) and

---

[15] Walthamstow Hall was founded in1838 as an all –girl inter –denominational mission school and home for the daughters of Christian missionaries. Originally situated in Walthamstow, by the time that Constance and her sisters attended the school it had moved to a site in Holly Bush Lane in Sevenoaks in 1882. The school was the first of its kind in the country and the daughters of all evangelical missionaries were received. The opening of the school coincided with the ground –breaking century for the recognition and education of young women, and "Pioneers of female education were a hard –headed, hard –working, idealistic and common-sense groups of middle –class, Christian women" (per Wikipedia). Its alumnae were to the forefront of women in academia.

lunched with the Williams family, walking extensively in the city with Ivy (to Cowley) and with Winter, before attending Christchurch cathedral and going home (home at the time presumably being the house maintained by her father at Chalfont road).

She qualified as a doctor in 1904 with a first from Oxford and a degree from London University. The medical profession in England had opened its doors (accidentally) to women in 1865 with the single qualification of Elizabeth Garrett Anderson (1836 –1917), which wasn't emulated for several years thereafter. So, by the time Constance passed her examination in 1904, there were fewer than 500 women practising in England. America was ahead of the UK by about 20 years, and an Englishwoman, Elizabeth Backwell, had qualified there in 1849. The role of women in the late nineteenth and early twentieth century in the medical profession is typified by affluent white women who tended to work in the colonies and were frequently evangelical. That is a fair description of Constance Cousins.

Between 1904 and 1911, she had spent time working as a doctor in an English hospital as encouraged by loving letters from her father in Madagascar. Like Ivy, it seems clear that she enjoyed the support of her family; she never considered any life other than as a medical missionary in India and was educated and supported with that aim in mind.

Constance applied to the London Missionary Society in 1911 to work as a medical missionary but was surprisingly rejected in the false belief that she suffered from epilepsy (which, in all likelihood, she did not).

Without the formal support of the society, she made her way to the Almora Sanitorium in India, run at the time by the Church of Scotland, and worked initially as an unpaid assistant. Almora is situated to the north of New Delhi in the Himalayan foothills and, at the time, was accessible only by means of a dandy (a boat –shaped carrier slung from poles and carried by bearers). Her mother's example in Madagascar and her own early years will have stood her in good stead for the experience.

Her letters home from Almora were regular and have been preserved in the Cousins Collection held in London by the School of Oriental and Asian Studies. The letters speak of a driven young woman impatient to do more. The hospital she worked in was a two –storey building with a veranda and housed twelve patients. It had a crude surgical capability. The clinic specialised in the treatment of tuberculosis, but Constance was dismayed by what she saw as over –medication and failure to pay attention to more fundamental needs such as diet, exercise, fresh air and a positive attitude. She addressed these by drawing up a series of regulations for the patients, including calling on patients to work in the hospital gardens as well as setting sewing targets for younger patients – she was clearly a believer in hard work being a virtue. I have felt in my research that Constance and Ivy shared many values and enjoyed each other's company very much.

She survived on a small stipend from her family; she worked long hours and spent four hours daily learning the local languages. She could speak Urdu and Hindi and engaged with the patients to perfect her studies.

The hospital at Almora, however, faced difficulties the year after her arrival. The place could be cold and damp, which was not conducive to recovery from tuberculosis; patients rebelled against her too –bracing regime, and a patient's death sapped her enthusiasm. But her ideas did work. There was a slow improvement. Constance introduced lengthy walks, the study of English, a choir and embroidery into the day's activities. Increasingly her correspondence shows a fascination with medicine and a secondary interest in missionary work.

Her efforts were noticed, and in 1913, the Church of Scotland offered her a salaried position in the Charteris Memorial Hospital in Kalimpong in North India. She was excited to work with the well –known Dr JA Graham. She moved to a 40 –bed hospital in Kalimpong, where she remained for the next ten years, working with 15,000 patients a year and being paid an annual salary of £140 – underlining the fact that only women from a reasonably wealthy background could afford to do this type of work. She had a two –mile horseback ride daily from her living quarters to the hospital and the same in the evening. As a woman, she received up to 50 patients a day as word got around the local female community that there was a woman doctor available to them. As well as working at the Charteris Hospital Constance worked at the St Andrew's Home for Eurasians, a children's hospital, and ran two district dispensaries some distance away. Trips to these dispensaries took a five –day ride by horseback to very simple facilities but were a source of delight for Constance, who seems chiefly to have enjoyed midwifery roles there.

Constance, like Ivy, was tall, and she was also angular and deeply suntanned from her regular horseback rides. The colleagues with whom she worked were dedicated and hardworking, rarely taking holidays, and tried to recreate aspects of their previous life in England around them in their furnishings and gardens.

In 1918 she was requested to help with the outbreak of a cholera epidemic in neighbouring Bhutan. No other doctor was available (or willing) to undertake the dangerous journey over the mountains. Constance duly set off with a hospital nurse as her only companion and became the first English woman to visit Bhutan. There, her success in resolving the cholera crisis led to an act of recognition from the king, who presented her with a banner to mark her achievement. On the return journey, she fell ill, and it is only due to the ministrations of her steadfast companion, Nurse Brodie, that she was able to return to India in safety.

In 1923 Constance left Kalimpong to return to Almora. She had fallen out with Dr James, and her health was suffering from the conditions at Kalimpong; an offer from Almora was a timely exit plan. At Almora, she became the superintendent of the sanitorium and remained in the post until her death 21 years later. Conditions were poor; the place was small and understaffed with meagre supplies. Its patients were mainly tuberculosis sufferers or lepers. Some things had improved – the sanitorium had now become accessible by car and received modest central government funding. Constance's salary was withdrawn in 1923, but this didn't affect her work: she possibly enjoyed freedom from the constraint imposed by being an employee of the Church of Scotland.

By 1939 Constance had established a hospital for Muslim women and children and Indian Christian girls and was seeing a satisfying recovery rate amongst her tuberculosis patients. Like her cousins and nieces, she championed the cause of the so –called "untouchables" and moved freely amongst the complicated caste system.

Her letter –writing home dwindled; letters that survive show a religious tolerance. She suffered from typhus at this time and lost weight, and developed a stoop. When she eventually retired, she received no pension and died shortly after giving up work of heart failure. She was buried at Almora.

Ivy and Constance frequently corresponded in their younger days; they shared values and supported each other with encouragement for their examination success.

Mabel Eliza (sometimes Elise) Cousins.

Mabel was a year older than Ivy and, although born in Madagascar, returned to England to attend the school for missionaries in Walthamstow Hall with her siblings. She studied medicine at London University and lived in the early 1900s in Oxford. Records of her attendance at London university give her address as 40, St Johns Street, Oxford (indicating that London University offered the equivalent of distance learning at that time) and show her as already married, and formerly Cousins with an MB obtained in 1898. She left for Borneo with her husband George Dexter Allen in about 1904, aged 28, where she worked as an eye doctor. The couple left Borneo in 1915, and she became a temporarily consulting physician at St Andrew's Medical Mission Hospital in Malaya in 1920. The couple were medical missionaries, and to enable them to work together as such, her husband took a course in medicine. Her husband predeceased her having returned on leave to the UK in 1929. Mabel Eliza never returned to the UK after this; she continued her work, remarried and spent her last years in Singapore and may have been there in 1942 when the Japanese invaded and her record ends.

Janet and Winifred Cousins.

Janet and Winifred, Ivy's nieces, were the daughters of Ivy's cousin Herbert Cousins, who spent much of his life in Jamaica working as a pioneering agriculturist. The girls saw for themselves the conditions of the locals and the impact of slavery and were anthropologists and novelists. Janet was a music student and novelist who wrote about the plight of slavery in Jamaica in her three novels. She also compiled the informal life of Constance Cousins. Winifred described herself as an anthropologist and was similarly engaged in anti –slavery and awareness –raising work – Ivy was her first referee in her application to Royal Holloway to read for a History degree. Neither married, and both received bequests under Ivy's will.

It was not only the Williams women who were inspirational or who demonstrated the pioneering drive to serve and robust intellect. There were also London based spurs of the family where the pioneering spirit and competency with the law were also in evidence.

John Williams

The famous missionary John Williams (1796 –1839) was a cousin several times removed. John was famous for his missionary work in Vanuatu; he was a practical man who built boats with his own hands and was highly charismatic. He was very successful in his missionary work in the South Seas. Several books have been written about him, and his portrait is in the National Portrait Gallery. He was martyred in 1829 when he was attacked (and allegedly eaten) by natives on the island of Erromango, where he had landed in the hope of converting the local population. To this day, the locals consider that this act brought bad luck to the island. My uncle Peter Prior visited the island a few years ago to see the site of the death. John and Ivy shared a common 3rd great grandfather in John Williams (1650 –1693), who was born in Coate (now Cote) as the first generation of Williams to be born in Oxfordshire after their removal from Wales.

Joshua Williams QC, Thomas Cyprian Williams and Sir Joshua Strange Williams.

Ivy was more closely related to the Williams lawyers in London and may have had contact with them whilst residing there and preparing for her Bar exams in 1921. Joshua Williams QC (1813 –1881) was a highly successful QC in London and the author of the leading text on land transactions. He was also a first – generation departee from Cote and, prior to his call by Lincoln's Inn, had practised as a certified conveyancer. His degree was from London University. In 1875, after a very successful career, he was appointed a professor of law of real and personal property at the Inns of Court by the Council of Legal Education. His "Principles of the Law of Real Property" (first as "Williams on Conveyancing") ran through 18 editions; he published extensively. His own children were to follow him into the law. His son, Thomas Cyprian Williams (1854 –1932), also a barrister, edited editions of his work from 1881. His son Sir Joshua Strange Williams (1837 –1915), was hailed as one of the great legal brains of his age. After a stellar career at Cambridge, where he won the chancellor's gold medal for legal studies, he was called to the Bar by Lincoln's Inn in 1859 but suffered from nerves and subsequently removed to New Zealand (during the gold rush) for his health and practised as a solicitor. He became prominent in local politics and, retiring from his solicitor's practice, became Land Registrar for the country (writing a handbook on the Land Transfer Acts) and subsequently a judge in Otago and then one of three new judges appointed to the supreme court of New Zealand. He was subsequently appointed chancellor of the University of Otago and was active in various charitable fields. He retired to England and was New Zealand's first permanent representative on the Privy Council.

It is perhaps both remarkable and predictable that the Williams lawyers were all specialists in land matters at a time when the law had many facets. Ivy herself gained her highest marks in the conveyancing exams. Finally – as the footnote to this work reveals in exploring Ivy's genealogy, the strands of her Welsh heritage are also awash with politicians, lawyers and judges.

Chapter 5
Women in Law – Ivy's personal battle; Failure to launch

This photo (like others of Ivy) was taken by the Oxford photographer William Forshaw who was active in Oxford between 1872 and 1905. The academic gown suggests that it may be a graduation picture from London university or a post –exam photo from Ivy's Oxford Exams. The writing is my grandfather's; interestingly, he referred to Ivy as "aunt", although they were, in fact, cousins. She was a little older and probably a great deal more confident.

Women had been attempting with little success to join the legal profession worldwide when Ivy completed her Legal education.

In 1860 Maria Susan Rye (1829 –1903) opened a law stationer in Portugal Street, Lincolns Inn Fields, to train about 20 female law clerks in the art of copying legal documents. She was the daughter of a solicitor, although she lacked the education afforded her brothers. She became aware of the disadvantage that this placed women under and became a campaigner for reform of the married women's property law and, more generally, for women's emancipation. Her stationer's office was founded under the auspices of the Society for Promoting the Employment of Women. It was a successful enterprise, but Maria became disillusioned about the impact such a small business could have on the problem of women's under –employment. Her focus thereafter switched to advocating emigration as a way of offering greater freedom of choice.

Elsewhere in the world, women were having a greater impact on the law. In Iowa, Arabella Babb Mansfield was admitted to the Bar in 1869, and by 1879 women were free to practice generally in the US; Ontario admitted Clara Brett Martin to the Bar that same year. In 1895 Finland and Sweden opened the profession to women, and two years later, New Zealand permitted Ethel Benjamin to practice. France admitted women in 1900, and in 1905 Victoria in Australia admitted Grata Flos Greig to the Bar; Norway opened the profession to women in 1904.

Progress was considerably slower in the UK.

In 1873 Janet Wood took a first in a special women's examination at Girton, becoming the first woman to complete a law degree (although, of course, women were not entitled to graduate and hold degrees until 1947 – lagging behind even their sisters in Oxford who acquired the right in 1920 –because of the tardiness of Cambridge in recognising women's entitlement to graduate). The same year Maria Grey and the Women's Education Union applied for permission to attend law lectures at Lincoln's Inn. The Council of Legal Education at the time permitted "gentlemen" generally to attend lectures upon payment of a fee. In the universities at the time, women were increasingly being permitted to attend lectures in an unofficial capacity. For that reason, Miss Grey and 92 other ladies petitioned Lincoln's Inn for like permission to attend. Perhaps predictably, Lincoln's Inn resolved at a Council meeting on 11 March 1873 that it *"is not expedient that Women should be admitted to the Lectures of the Professors appointed by the Council of Legal Education"*. An application by a Miss Day in 1891 to become a licensed conveyancer to the same Inn was rejected on the entirely circular grounds of there being no precedent for such an application.

A more commercial approach by Eliza Orme (1848 – 1937) was to set up a law office in Chancery Lane in 1875 under the name of Orme and Richardson (Richardson being a friend - Mary Richardson). Three years earlier, she had been accepted as a pupil to John Savill Vaizey in Lincolns Inn, having completed a law degree at London University. Her aspiration was to become a *"conveyancer under the Bar"*, which was blocked. Instead, her work took the form of devilling for conveyancing counsel and patent agents. She took an increasing interest in politics and was a founding member of the Women's Liberal Foundation in 1887; she obtained a law degree in 1888.

Women's progress at the universities developed with the arrival of the extraordinary Cornelia Sorabji (1866 –1954) as a graduate of Bombay University in Oxford in 1892, as the first woman to read law at Oxford at Sommerville College. Her attendance at Oxford was "crowd –funded", including a contribution from Florence Nightingale. She was an active practising lawyer in India as a legal advisor representing women and minors in provincial courts, although her admission as a barrister in India was deferred until 1924, by which time she had helped hundreds of women and orphans fight legal battles. Cornelia was a contemporary of Ivy's. Alice Adams became the first woman undergraduate in law at Oxford at this time.

In 1900 permission was sought by Margaret Howie Strang Hall to sit the Scottish solicitor's preliminary examinations. She had been employed as a clerk by a local law office in Dunoon and had the offer of an apprenticeship at those offices were her application to be successful. Her application was refused by the Society of Law Agents, whereupon Margaret petitioned the Court of Sessions for authority to enrol for the examinations. The matter went unusually to a full court hearing with representations from both sides and useful precedent from other professions and from abroad. Perhaps unsurprisingly, it was ultimately unsuccessful, there being no "power" to so order, and the expression "persons" [entitled to present themselves for examination] not being extended to women. This was a foreshadowing of the notorious Bebb litigation\ in England in 1914.

It was against this unpromising background that Ivy completed her legal education and turned to the profession. That Ivy's early academic success did not initially result in her being called to the Bar confounded her original intention to practice. She was amongst many other women held at arm's length by the male profession until after the war. Her early intentions, however, were well publicised and radical.

Ivy's academic success as a schoolgirl (albeit home tutored) was being reported in the 1990s. In 1993 the Oxford Journal reported local success in Oxford Local examinations – Ivy came third, having been prepared with her brother by tutors in the under 19 class although she was only 15. It is reported that she passed Latin, German, English grammar, history, arithmetic, Euclid algebra, quadratic equations, mechanics, hydrostatics and botany. She headed the honours list in German, obtained a distinction in French (she was fluent in the language and was later to participate in the Hague conference in French) and, as a result of these credentials, was awarded a Certificate of exemption for women enabling her to proceed directly to the University honours exam in law and jurisprudence expressed to be the *" best school in the world to study law"*, to prepare for London University LLB as London (unlike Oxford) granted law degrees to ladies, whilst Oxford only allowed them to take exams not degrees.

On 19 September 1994, The Oxfordshire Weekly News reported that Ivy had taken ten exams set by the

University of London Board and had achieved her higher certificate at recent examinations of Oxford and Cambridge University schools board in German, French, English, History, arithmetic, algebra, Euclid, mechanics and hydrostatics with distinction in French and German whilst still considerably younger than the intended age of the participant.

In 1895 local records show George St. Swithin Williams' address as 17, King Edward Street (possibly incorrectly) and St. Swithin Williams (the name he tended to use professionally) at 12, King Edward Street; Winter is listed as working at 12, King Edward Street profession barrister at law – this is premature. He was at the time still an undergraduate and did not seek admission to Inner Temple until 1896, being called in 1899. The 1903 records show 4 inhabitants at 12, King Edward Street – 1. Oxon and Berks Bank, 2. St. Swithin Williams solicitor; 3. George St. Swithin Williams and 4. Winter Williams barrister.

Whilst Oxford was starting to open its doors to women with the establishment of specific colleges for women, a number of women students were known as "Home – Students" and were based in their own homes in Oxford or lodged there. By 1896 there were 46 Home –Students, and this category of student was formally adopted by the AEW council in 1898. From 1894 the Society of Home – Students was run from Mrs Johnson's home at 8, Merton Street at her own expense. Bertha Johnson (1846 –1927) was a remarkable woman in the early development of women at Oxford. Whilst slow to accept the case for full admission of the women to degrees at Oxford (although ultimately amongst the cohort in 1920 that collected degrees), she was a steadfast supporter of women's education and took a pastoral role in the facilitation of their progress often at her own personal expense. It was to the Home Students under the wing of Mrs Johnson that, at the age of 19 in 1896, Ivy Williams started her legal studies. It was a time of increasing agitation amongst women for equal rights with men (for example, in1897 National Union of Women's suffrage was founded), something that the Liberal Williams family would have supported.

Ivy's brother Winter had already commenced his legal studies at Corpus Christi College in Oxford, which he completed in 1898 and then enrolled as a student at Inner Temple; he was called to the Bar in 1899.

Whilst his children were deep in their legal studies, George St. Swithin was involved in money lending locally[16]and probably also worked as a solicitor and property developer. He seems to have employed at least two clerks to assist him, Anson Lester Boddington and Albert Coppock and the book of business identifies the "leader" in each lending transaction that is then checked by a second person. The initials of the second person do not match those of the clerks. George was less active than

---

[16] For example on 24.2.1896 George St Swithin Williams of Merton House gentleman loaned £40 to Richard Adam Davis of Chequers Inn Wheatley against property in High Street Wheatly; On 5 March 1897 he loaned £560 to Mr Morris and wife of Royal Standard Headington against mortgage of land at New Headington and 4 houses on it – loan repaid quickly; and on 2.12 (or 12.3) 1897 George St Swithin of Bushey Close (this is the first and only record I can find of him treating this address as his residence) lent £50 –The bill book does record a loan on 12 March to R England of 82 Abingdon Rd.

the others, but all large loans were made by him. The book is a meticulous record of all transactions, recording repayments and security taken, something George would do himself to streamline the business. He was able to lend up to £1,000 at the time, and from family records, Ivy and her cousins, the Priors, also made loans and received interest for these. George's largest loans were to Harry Neville Prior and whilst these seem to have been repaid they give the impression that Harry Neville may have overextended himself – there are smaller loans made to his wife independently of him which rather supports this impression.

On her arrival as a student, Ivy would have been able to attend lectures, but a central meeting point for the Home Students was initially at Bertha Johnson's house until, in 1899, the Home-Students were given access to a common room at 131, High Street.

Ivy was living at the time at 12, King Edward Street; however, records show that her father was then particularly active in business and acquired Sunnyside – a significant plot in Cowley – where Ivy was later to live. He also started to pass property to Ivy directly (possibly as part of some form of estate planning). For example, he conveyed Manse land in Cowley to Ivy in two parts on 8th May, 1899 and 2nd June, 1899. It is also possible that her father was becoming unwell at this time and passing responsibility for business matters to her.

Ivy was active in student matters. In June 1900, she was elected President of Oxford Students Debating Society (presumably a society for women students) and known to have taken part in a moot in which she prosecuted a poacher. That year she took the 2nd class in jurisprudence. She was not able to collect her degree until 1920, however, due to the restrictions on women students. Her aunt and uncle, the Bakers, died at this time, although Ivy does not seem to have been very close to them.

The turn of the century marked a number of significant events. It marked the formation of the Labour party and, shortly thereafter, the death of the elderly Queen Victoria. Ivy, now aged 24, solidified her Oxford exam results with a degree from London University (London has a more enlightened approach to women students). Towards the end of 1901, the Yorkshire Post recorded the results of the London University LLB examinations with the pass list 2nd division listing Ivy Williams of Oxford University Home students and private tuition. In 1902 she was awarded the BCL and subsequently the LLD from London in 1903.

Opinions differ as to whether Ivy was amongst three women who applied in 1903 for admission to the Inns of Court. The archivist at Inner Temple was unable to find any record of this, but newspaper reports at the time suggest that she did indeed apply unsuccessfully to Inner Temple in about 1904, although it is possible that she never made a formal application. The archivist observes wryly that the absence of a record – whilst usually irregular – may simply reflect the Inns of Court's view at the time that women's applications were too frivolous to warrant recording.

On 26 February 1903, The London Evening Standard reported that Ivy was to raise the question of women's rights to practise law as one of four successful candidates

85

for the LLD at London – and the first to pass at both universities (viz Oxford and London), it reported her 2nd class pass of the Oxford Bachelor of Law exam (for which no firsts were awarded) and that she came second in the London University list. It seems that this was not the completion of her course(s) as a report of 25 November 1903 in the Evening Mail published a pass list for LLD Common Law and Equity, which included Ivy as an Oxford Home Student. It confirmed that she intended to apply to Inner Temple and go to parliament if need be – and that she aspired to practice as a *"poor man's lawyer"* without fees. It describes her as very clear and articulate. She was said to favour running a Legal dispensary like a local university offered. In this, she was referring to a project of the recently established Mansfield College, Oxford, in London's East End.

The report was echoed towards the end of the year when on 19 December 1903, the Law Journal identified a *"doughty champion"* for women's entry into the profession – again, it is reported that she intended to act as a poor man's lawyer without fees – and stated that she is accustomed to public speaking. At this point in time, the only record of Ivy having experience of public speaking is the references from her time at Oxford, where she was an active member of the debating society and had conducted a moot. Later in life, she was to speak regularly to a gathering of congregations and local political meetings. Subsequently, they reported her message that the legal profession *"will have to admit us or we will form a separate profession as outside lawyers"*.

News of this reached America – the Boston journal reported Ivy as being interested in Sunday school work and as being wholly philanthropic. It reported her intended application to Inner Temple and that if that failed that she proposed to lay her case before Parliament. By this time, women were accepted into the profession in America, and the report also referred to women being allowed to practice in Europe, identifying England as well behind the curve.

On 26 December 1903, The London Daily News picked up on the comment that Ivy might practice "*outside the law*" and questioned how this would be possible in practice. For example, how would there be any costs recovery in successful cases for her clients, and how would they gain access to the courts? What would these "outlaw" lawyers be called? If "legal advisors" they could do non–contentious work. The threat to ignore the establishment was seen as a threat to ignore the "*etiquette which at present binds the existing profession*" and was criticised as unlikely to be productive. This overlooked the fact that Ivy did not propose to charge for her work, so she would have no need to collect costs – but clearly, such a process would not be sustainable when it became necessary to fund the legal work performed by lady lawyers.

Amidst all the anticipation, however, Ivy's home life was about to be devastated. On 27 March 1903, her brother Winter, who had an interest in bookbinding, and had set up a printing press at Stock Street in Cowley, suffered a major accident losing much of his right hand. Four months later, he died unexpectedly of a stomach infection at his home in All Hallows, the site of the Sunnyside house.

Women who had at the time applied to the Inns of the Court were at this point launching appeals against refusals. In December 1903, Bertha Cave failed to appeal to Gray's Inn's refusal to admit her in spite of having the support of two masters. Her appeal went to the House of Lords, where she appeared for herself. On 12 January 1904, the Southern Echo reported applications to two Inns of Court by Ivy and Miss Pankhurst and opined that a woman's place was not in the law.

Bertha Cave's application to Gray's Inn was made at a time when she (like Christabel Pankhurst, who also failed in her application at this time) had yet to matriculate in a university course. Whilst this may not have been an impediment to admission to an Inn of Court, it certainly placed her in an uncertain category as to quality. Her appeal to the Lord Chancellor seems to have been doomed before it was heard. She appeared on behalf of herself and another unnamed lady student who had also applied to Gray's Inn. She was invited to speak *"if she wished,"* and although the proceedings were in private from an interview that she gave afterwards, the thrust of her argument seems to have been that there were other women in Europe – Holland, for example – who was admitted to practice; that she did not seek to take from the male Bar any significant part of their work, was content to be a "humble" counsel and had no aspirations to the bench. The dismissing judgment of the Lord Chancellor was given almost as soon as she had completed speaking, and apparently, the Law Lords found her very presence amusing.

It might have been a better strategy for the women who were at the time seeking admission to the profession to have coordinated their approach. Of the several women "in the mix," two were eminently better qualified to seek admission. Both Ivy and Eliza Orme were at the time qualified as lawyers in so far as they held law degrees – Ivy's of the highest quality. Ivy was one of the only two applicants in the country to hold a doctorship in Law from London and also to have completed the examinations in jurisprudence in Oxford. She was famously well qualified and well connected. Ivy seems to have held back her application pending seeing how Bertha's proceeded. Having seen the failure of Bertha both before the Benchers and subsequently on Appeal to the courts, her options were limited by the unfortunate precedent created. A better –qualified candidate with stronger and more fully researched arguments (for example, pointing not only to precedents from abroad but, for example, to the medical profession in the United Kingdom where women were full participants and their quasi –judicial role as factory inspectors) might possibly have fared better (there was, in particular, a comment about Bertha that she was not a "Girton girl" suggesting that the backing on ancient university might have been of assistance). In the event of that unhelpful precedent, Ivy was left only with recourse to the court of public opinion and to Parliament to clear the way for women to the Bar – something that took 18 years. That she felt that the lack of qualification may have been a determining factor in the refusal of the Inns of

Courts to Bertha at the time is borne out by subsequent events concerning a debate at Lincoln's Inn.

The matter continued to occupy the minds of the profession, and in January 1904, the Lincoln's Inn debate took place hosted by the Union Society of London on the subject of the admission of ladies to the Bar. This was widely advertised as an event at which Bertha Cave, Christabel Pankhurst and Ivy would all speak against the motion which called for women to be denied access to the legal profession. Although unable to attend, Ivy wrote to suggest an amendment to the generality of the topic, suggesting that women should first have a law degree to be admitted. This was not only a response to a concern that the profession might become diluted by the "rush" of underqualified women but also met the concern that seemed at the time to be circulating that women lawyers would have the effect of diminishing the fees that the male members of the profession might earn.

In spite of seeing how Bertha had fared, on 15 January 1904, The Englishwoman's Review announced that Ivy would (again) put the admission of women to the test in Inner Temple as poor man's lawyers under the auspices of some charitable organisation in Oxford (a further reference to the Mansfield House project) and on 23 January 1904 The Solicitor's Journal also picked up the story. It seems likely that it was a necessary first step to seek admission and fail before taking the matter further – in Ivy's case, she promised to seek the intervention of Parliament rather than the doomed route already tested by Bertha Cave.

Ivy's seriousness about applying to become a barrister can be seen from the press campaign that she seems to have undertaken in 1903 and a little thereafter in spite of the personal tragedy that engulfed the family. Whilst the reports are very similar in their content, they do differ sufficiently to suggest that she gave a series of interviews and not that one interview was subsequently taken up and used selectively. Her cousin Ethel Constance Cousins, at this point, had got a first in her medical exams in Oxford and was looking forward to working in a hospital (she worked in English hospitals from 1904 –1911 before travelling overseas as a medical missionary). How frustrating this must have been to Ivy to see the medical profession clearing the way for women whilst the law remained obdurate. It was at this point that the Oxford Suffrage Society was formed.

On 1 April 1904, The Dundee Evening Post reported (prematurely – but it was April 1st...) that Ivy was about to be called as the only woman who was fully qualified. It referred to an interview she had given. In it, she explained,

> *"Like my brother, the later Mr Winter Williams, who was called to the Bar at Inner Temple in 1899, I have been educated expressly for the legal profession and have been studying continuously for 8 years. My father, who is a solicitor, considered that the courses of law study prescribed by the two universities of Oxford and London constitute when combined, an equally perfect legal education. They embrace every branch of law, and the seven successive law examinations of these two universities lead up to one*

another and dovetail. I believe I am the only person who has passed all the law exams of the two universities of Oxford and London – 6 of the 7 [are] more difficult than the Bar examinations.... "

It is interesting to note the emphasis that Ivy placed on her training and qualifications as distinguishing her application. I suspect that she already feared that the path had been closed off by the previous failed attempts but hoped perhaps to make a distinct case for admission based on legal merit.

In anticipation of Ivy still being about to practice on 9 April 1904, The Queen referred to an article by Constance Barnicoat in "Girls Realm" where Ivy was quoted as stating,

> *"My object in becoming a barrister is to be a poor man's lawyer. I do not seek pecuniary gain; of that, I have no need. In connection with some great charitable institutions I hope to conduct a "legal dispensary" similar to the "Poor Man's Lawyer" at Mansfield University Settlement Canning Town."*[17]

---

[17] The article may have been lifted in part from a full interview given by Ivy in December 1903 to The Oxford Chronicle although the various publications at the time record similar but not identical sentiments suggesting that Ivy was indeed wooing the Press as part of her campaign at the time.
"Transcript of an article in the Oxford Chronicle December 2003
*"An **Oxford Lady's legal lore**.*
Interview with Miss Ivy Williams
A champion of women's rights.
The recent decision of the Judges against the admission of women to act as Barristers has once more directed public attention to the fact that law is the sole remaining profession at the present time closed to the female sex. The question is of peculiar interest in Oxford, as Miss Ivy Williams of 12, King

Edward St, was one of the four successful candidates in the last Doctor of Laws examination.

In an interview with a representative of the Oxford Chronicle yesterday Dr Ivy Williams, an attractive young lady of six and twenty, spoke vivaciously and freely of her training for a profession which apparently presented insurmountable difficulties.

"How was it," inquired the interviewer, "You came to take up the study of law?"

"As the daughter of a solicitor it was my early ambition, and as proof of fitness to be a lawyer I have passed seven law examinations in the Universities of Oxford and London. I have studied law for eight years. Many men have passed all the law examinations of Oxford University, and many others have passed all the law examinations of London University, but may I say that I am the only person who has ever passed all the law examinations of both these Universities? Before specialising in study of law I obtained eight certificates of examinations from the universities of Oxford, Cambridge and London, paying particular attention to Latin, German, French, history, mathematics, and natural science."

"What was the course of study you pursued?"

"I have been educated exclusively by distinguished tutors in the Universities of London and Oxford, deriving especial benefit from Mr G B Burnham law tutor of University Collage."

"Your brother, the late Mr Winter Williams, I believe, was Called?"

"Yes, he was a member of the Inner Temple, and was called to the Bar in 1899. I have been educated on the same lines – studying jurisprudence and the principles of legislation, the early history of legal institutions, Roman law, whole of the law of England and international law, public and private."

"You have taken a much wide range of subjects than is ordinarily the case?"

"That is so. A man begins to practise long before he is gone to the extent of this training, and consequently has fewer opportunities for study. The course of legal study in the two Universities of Oxford and London forms an ideal legal education. The Oxford Law Preliminary Examination is an introduction to the Intermediate Bachelor of Laws Examination in London University. That examination prepares the way for the final B.A. examination in the Oxford Honours School of Jurisprudence. This is followed by the still wider range of subjects required for the Final Bachelor of Laws examination in London University. When this has been successfully faced the Oxford BCL, examination presents no difficulties. The course it crowned by the London Doctor of Laws examination probably most difficult Law Examination in the world."

"And how did you fare in the Oxford Bachelor of Civil Law examination?"

"I gained a second class; no first class being awarded. At the London Bachelor of Laws examination, I was bracketed second in the honours list, and in the Oxford BA examination I obtained a second class in the Honours School of Jurisprudence."

"I understand you intend champion right women to become lawyers; what is your plan of campaign?"

"I hope to bring the influence of public opinion and the Press to bear on the subject. Having passed all these examinations and given evidence of qualification in the only way open to me, why should I be deBarred from

93

At this stage, as noted above, both Ivy and Eliza Orme had passed law exams and received their degrees from London University, and Ivy's comments about the path she proposed to follow may well have been intended to pave the way for her own application, meeting concerns about un or underqualified women rushing in and resulting in lowering of fees – in that she would charge none and would be fully qualified. It also allowed her to promote the doing of "good works" as her driving motivation at a time when philanthropy was highly valued. The journalist who took up Ivy's story, Constance Barnicoat, was a famous New Zealander mountaineer and intrepid promoter of women's achievements in her own right.[18]Their classical educational background, linguistic

---

participating in the practical work of an honourable profession? I desire to see the subject thoroughly discussed before applying to the Inner Temple for admission as a student for the Bar, and, if necessary, I intend to appeal to Parliament itself. I wish to emphasise that it is not my intention to practise with a view to pecuniary profit, but as a poor man's lawyer without fees. For some time, past there has been a movement in this direction in connection with the University Settlements in London, which are known as "Legal Dispensaries". I propose to introduce a similar system under the auspices of some charitable organisation in Oxford"

Least the foregoing record of academic successes create a wrong impression, for it is only fair to state that Dr. Ivy Williams is no "blue stocking". She thoroughly enjoys outdoor exercises, and particularly riding, cycling, tennis, skating it is also an expert diver and swimmer."

[18] Constance by 1904 had climbed several of the most challenging peaks in Europe, had been home educated and was a strong horsewoman. She had a classical education in New Zealand where her parents kept in touch from their farm with the outside world through European periodicals. She went to Canterbury College where she obtained her BA excelling in English and worked initially as a secretary for one of the country's politicians. She left New Zealand for England in 1897 and won prizes at secretarial College for her shorthand, French and German; she could also speak Italian and Spanish. She was exposed to politics on the wider global stage as secretary and interpreter at the Hague Peace conference in 1899. She had a deep religious conviction. She was known to be blunt and outspoken. She married a Romanian Jewish journalist in 1911 and lived much of her life thereafter in Switzerland where she provided a listening post for newspapers worldwide on the developing political situation.

skills and political and religious convictions were strikingly similar.

Shortly after, on 25 May 1904 at London University degree day, Ivy received the loudest cheer as one of two recipients of LLD. The Wigan Observer remarked how women were well represented at the degree ceremony.

However, the tide changed, and by 28 May 1904, the Illustrated London News reported that Ivy was one of only two Doctors of Law but had been refused admission to the Inns of Court to prepare for legal practice, "*although the degree she holds in far beyond the requirements of the average barrister*". This suggests that, in all probability, her application was made sometime between December 1903 and May 1904 and failed. By 1904 Ivy had given up, it seems, the hope of admission to the profession by way of appeal to the courts. It may be, however, that at least at first, she was contemplating acting "outside" the law drawing on the template of the Mansfield House project. Her long interview of December 1903 suggested that she would set up a similar practice in Oxford, and indeed several "Legal Dispensaries" existed in London and elsewhere at the time, all based on the Mansfield House model[19]. This had been set up in Canning Town in the East

---

[19] The Mansfield settlement was the project of Mansfield College Oxford, a College founded in the nineteenth century by Congregationalists. Founded originally in Birmingham in 1838 as Spring Hill College it removed to Oxford in 1886 and was renamed Mansfield College after George and Elizabeth Mansfield, the original College's largest benefactors.
Canning Town had quickly become known as an area where people were committed to improving conditions for themselves and others. The area became the birthplace of the Labour party with the election of Kier Hardie as a Labour MP in 1892
The Settlement movement, following on from a slightly earlier religious movement, was founded by the Reverend Samuel Barnett in the late 19th

End of London. It is impossible to tell whether Ivy had visited the settlement or even worked there but certainly, meetings in Oxford at the university at the time described and introduced the system to the public. The fundamentals and origins of the movement – Congregationalist and Liberal, Oxford instigated – seem completely aligned with Ivy's own philosophy; she was at the time in regular contact with her two cousins who were studying medicine and based in Oxford with a view to going out into the world as medical missionaries – that way was not so open for a lawyer, but this route would have been a natural one for Ivy to consider as an equivalent way to do service.

---

century on the basis that personal involvement was central to tackling poverty: giving money was not enough. Rather, educated people — the Settlements were usually linked to a university or public school — were encouraged to 'settle' in areas of social deprivation and to work alongside fellow residents to improve the quality of life for everyone. The East End of London was recognized as being a place where Settlements could play an important role, and Barnett opened the first, Toynbee Hall near Petticoat Lane in Whitechapel, in 1884.

In 1884 Frederick William Newland, an Oxford graduate and Congregational Church Minister, then began a ministry in Canning Town. He invited pairs of students to work with him for two weeks at a time during their holidays, and this created a link between Canning Town and Oxford University. This led, on 21 May 1890, to the inauguration of the Mansfield Settlement at a meeting at Mansfield College, Oxford. Percy Alden, then a theology student, agreed to be the Settlement's first warden — later he became Mayor of West Ham, then an MP, and he was eventually knighted in 1933.

Mansfield Settlement provided a range of social services when state provision was virtually non-existent. One of the first volunteers, the barrister Frank Tillyard, ran a free legal clinic on one evening a week. This became known as 'The Poor Man's Lawyer' and was widely copied by other Settlements. The concept for the settlements was radical for its time and extended into social clubs, shops and accommodation for those unable to afford their own, and depended on the involvement of established wealthy institutions becoming directly involved – not only did Oxford University support the project financially, it sent its own to work there. Similarly, Malvern School was to take up the challenge as did the Congregational Church.

In 1904 Ivy did not press for formal recognition, nor (so far as it is possible to tell) did she immediately seek to work as a poor man's lawyer. The reasons seem to be mainly personal.

Whilst she was completing her studies in 1903, her brother Winter first was seriously injured in a factory accident and then died of a serious infection a few months later, as reported above. Winter and Ivy were very close. She referred to him often and, in due course, founded a significant scholarship in his name at Oxford. He seems to have been a formidable man and a tragic loss at such an early age. He was a Liberal activist, parish councillor, candidate for parliament, talented sportsman and military reservist and was referred to as a *"walking encyclopaedia and paragon of all the virtues"* in his obituary. He was a regular correspondent on political matters in the newspapers. He also set up a printing press in Stock Street, Cowley (probably off Temple Road in Cowley, where he had a residence at All Hallows in Barracks Road, now Hollow Way – subsequently donated by Ivy to the church), which was ultimately taken over by the Church Army (and in all likelihood published philanthropic or religious tracts) and owned a typewriter (which came to Ivy and then to her cousin Percy Prior in due course). He clearly took a deep interest in the welfare of his employees – that concern leading to him losing part of his right hand in an accident where he chose to perform a dangerous printing manoeuvre himself rather than risk any of his staff. His accident occurred in March 1903, and he was treated at the Radcliffe, exhibiting great personal bravery. He was to die after three days of infection in July of that year at All Hallows in Barrack Road Cowley, with his father present at the death.

Her father also seems to have been ill at this time (his death certificate refers to cancer of the liver for 4 months as the cause of death, but the illness seems to have been longer in reality). By 1904 (from letters sent to her cousins), Ivy was with her mother in Karlsbad, taking muddy baths whilst her father recuperated. Karlsbad was at the time a popular spa town visited by thousands in Bohemia. The visit was doubtless to try to find a cure for her father, which sadly it did not achieve. As part of the trip, the family also visited Bournemouth, where in June Ivy listened to the Dan Godfrey Band, and to Vienna, where Ivy attended a concert with the wife of a local professor and reported seeing a wonderful rainbow.

In spite of these attempts to find a cure, on 19 September 1904, George St. Swithin Williams died. Ivy was 27 – she and her mother were alone in the world. The obituary describes St. Swithin as "*of London and Highgate*". This is likely to be a reference to a house that Ivy was subsequently to use in Highgate at Nassington Road, where her mother eventually died. It seems the family acquired this at some time, although records suggest that it was left to others from time to time. The obituary records that George St. Swithin had travelled to Germany in the hope of a cure with his wife and had returned to Oxford on 10 September very unwell and, after a short walk on the 11th September, had fallen into a steep decline. It was reported that he had been seriously ailing for some time and was greatly affected by the death of his son the previous year. He was remembered as an Old Volunteer and one of the first 100 who joined the force in 1860 – which seems to be a reference to a local militia. One account refers to a small family funeral at which an anonymous wreath in gratitude for his "kindness" was in place. His will, which is drafted in familiarly trenchant tones consistent with his correspondence with various newspapers, warns all beneficiaries against any challenge to his wishes. It left an estate valued at just under £80,000 (about £10.3 million today), which does not include *inter vivos* gifts of land already made. He made life provisions for his wife and sister Martha Wallis Prior (she of the feckless but charming husband) and to a Mrs Emily Horn (in recognition of her kindness to his mother and to his family) and bequests to 22 relatives. The residue, which was considerable, he left to Ivy.

After his death, Ivy seems to have pursued a political role (perhaps mindful of her promise to seek assistance from Parliament if her route to the Bar was barred by the courts) as well as handling the extensive business interests of her father and brother and suffering from a period of ill health.

Chapter 6
Politics

Shortly after her father's death Ivy and her mother seem to have completed their removal to Sunnyside, a new house in Cowley possibly originally inhabited by Winter (sometimes referred to as a farm). It may be that at this time (as speculated above), she spent time at Highfield, as recorded in the records at St Anne's.

Information about Ivy's activities at this time refers to local organisations and also to a period of ill health.[20]

Ivy set about arranging her domestic affairs – and towards the end of 1905, advertised for a

> "*Superior General Servant or Lady Help wanted, by 4th week of October for new house Sunnyside, Cowley. Must be reliable, clean, good –tempered and capable – apply to Ivy Williams 12 King Edward Street.*"

Whilst Ivy and her mother did move to Sunnyside in 1905, the lease on the house at King Edward Street was retained, and business seems to have continued from that address until Ivy eventually sold the lease in 1927.

---

[20] For example, on 27.5.05 "The Queen – Oxford notes" reported a bazaar at the Town Hall to clear debts on the Wesley Hall and Schools recently built in Cowley road and that on children's day 90 little girls presented posies to Ivy

Ivy completed her removal from Central Oxford to Cowley by October 1905. From that time forward, she invested time in the local politics of the area of Cowley – a new development where her brother had previously had both a small business (the printing press) and had been a parish councillor. He also had a residence at "All Hallow" in Barracks Road, subsequently renamed Hollow Way. All Hallows seems to have been the name of a Congregational manse where ministers of the local church lived but may have been part of the Sunnyside Estate, which ran to 50 acres. In due course, Ivy was to gift title to that property to the church absolutely.

In her time, Ivy was also to become a parish councillor, a stalwart of local church and children's religious education, a supporter of the local football team and a representative on various wartime committees.

The Williams historically and in Ivy's immediate family had always been interested in local affairs and politics generally. Her ancestors in Cote had formed several of the village's "Sixteen", her grandfather Adin had been a member of various local committees, her father was a regular correspondent in the newspapers on matters of national interest, and her brother Winter had been intended to be a Liberal candidate in national elections. Her financial advisor and uncle, Charles Ewers, was also a prominent local political figure – he had returned from Sheffield to Oxford with a new wife and young family in about 1895 and lived in Hurst Road in Cowley; he had taken an active role in local politics being an officer of the East Ward Liberal Association and pioneer of the East Ward Liberal Club.

It is unlikely that Ivy's political ambitions extended beyond local politics, and they regularly merged with her evangelical bent (something she shared with her cousins, the Cousins family) and with the Temperance society of which, like her father and immediate family, she was a firm supporter. In later life, she was able to offer much to the nation through her work at the Hague Conference and as a member of the Advisory Committee on the Deportation of Aliens, but these honours came to her late in life and after her call to the Bar and the publicity that that afforded her. In her younger days, immediately prior to the outbreak of the First World War, Ivy concentrated on carrying on the work done by her family in their stead and in being vigorously involved with her immediate community. This was at a time when it seems that she was suffering some personal illness that restricted her ability to do perhaps as much as she would have liked.

Ivy was a member of the South Oxfordshire Liberal women's association. Around the time of her move to Cowley, she addressed the membership, speaking about her Liberal roots.

On 6th October 1905, the Oxford Chronicle Reading Gazette reported on a meeting of the South Oxfordshire Liberal women's association. At this meeting, Ivy had spoken on *"Why I am a liberal"* as part of the management. The reasons she gave for being a liberal related to her family and their political beliefs; she stated that her father and grandfather (who she never knew) were *"never so happy"* as when working for the liberal cause. She referred to the fact that her brother Winter had been offered the local seat but had eventually refused. Most importantly, she reported that she had liberal beliefs, which she listed as women having equal legal and political rights and equal opportunities with men. The abolition of *"female slavery"* and the need to allow women to become MPs. She emphasized her temperance credentials and her belief in the rights of parents to educate and bring up children in their own sect. She spoke of the wider opportunities for higher education and Old age pensions that she thought essential. She concluded by confirming that she had, at that stage, only had one year to consider her political leanings, and these were the things that she had distilled in that year. At that meeting, the Liberal MP Philip Morrell (1870 –1943) was in attendance. He referred to the importance of Ivy in his speech. Morrell was the son of a local solicitor, and his grandfather had been President of St John's College and Vice –Chancellor of the University of Oxford. Whilst his grandfather had also been a man of the church, parallels with Ivy's own family end there, the Morells having made their fortune in brewing. He had been elected MP for Henley in 1906 as the only non –Conservative MP for that constituency. The event was chaired by Lady Ottoline Morrell (his wife) – the famous pacifist and attended by Alice Garland of the Women's Liberal Federation 1862 – 1939 – an OBE, suffragist and liberal party politician who stood unsuccessfully for parliament several times.

These persons were not obvious allies of Ivy. Not only did the Morrells represent the evils of alcohol, but they had an open marriage, and Phillip Morrell had several illegitimate children who his wife cared for; he struggled with his mental health. Ottoline had been a history student at Somerville College at the same time as Ivy was a Home –Student. They were as different as chalk and cheese. Ivy was a studious and ambitious law student with a healthy interest in outdoor pursuits; Ottoline was a literary hostess famed for her love affairs. In the time of war, she and her husband became famous pacifists, whereas Ivy's family were reservists. Ottoline was extravagant and financially irresponsible; Ivy was prudent, generous and meticulous in her financial affairs. But politics makes strange bedfellows, and Ivy's ambition at the time seems to forge this (and other) unexpected relationships.

On a smaller stage, on 28th February 1906, the Oxford Weekly News reported on the annual Oxfordshire Sunday School Convention at the Methodist Free Church attended by various non –conformists, at which Ivy was in the chair. She spoke about the controversy of how to teach religious education, as to which she considered it essential not to interfere with the views of the parents. The reports on finances and school visits given later at the convention included the comment that "*one of the most pleasing features of the year has been the kindness of the trustees of the Williams' bequest*" (the trustees were Ivy and the Rev James Robertson) which had paid for books and the publication of the weekly chronicle. Perhaps surprisingly, Ivy was not named on the list of elected officers.

Within six months of her removal to Cowley, Ivy was obliged to advertise again for a new servant. Perhaps having had a bad experience with her original choice, the new advertisement specifies a mature person with sober manners as a necessity. On 23 May 1906, she advertised for

"LADY HELP or superior SERVANT required to manage housework where help is given – must be total abstainer, clean, energetic, reliable and obliging. Over 30 preferred. Good salary for competence. Sunnyside."

On 27 June 1906, Ivy was present at the Oxford and District Christian Endeavour Union, where an address by Dr F E Clark – founder and President of the World Christian Endeavour Union, was given.

On 13 July 1906, the Oxford Chronicle and Reading Gazette reported on the annual al fresco fete and sale of work for the Congregational Church held on 12 July 1906 at Westwood House, Thame. Ivy had opened the fete in the rain and made a speech about doing God's work.

On 25th August 1906, the Oxford journal reported on the East Ward (the ward where Charles Ewers was active) Allotments show. Ivy gave out awards and made a speech encouraging those who grew produce on the allotments.

Later in the year, on 9 November 1906, the Luton Reporter reported on a Temperance Reform rally held at the famous Plait Halls in Luton in a downpour. The rally featured the Rec Canon Hicks of Manchester and Ivy (wrongly described as a *"lady medico from the classic City of Oxford"*) and drew a big audience. The then Mayor of Luton, Rev Henry Coate, declared that he had been "dry" for 20 years. Ivy:

"A tall lady with fair hair attired in a black costume humorously described herself as a little gun which was to be fired before the cannon spoke"

She described medical research in support of temperance, perhaps drawing on advice from her medically qualified cousins. From the legal perspective, she spoke of looking into the ability to exclude alcohol in neighbourhoods, of Sunday closing, control of clubs, abolition of bar maids, shorter hours of sale –all things she saw as a moderate program towards prohibition. She was 29 years old.

The following year 1907, the Somerville suffrage society was founded (after 1907, Oxford suffragists were represented at large NUWSS and WSPU marches in London). In spite of Ivy's threats to take on the establishment if they would not admit women, and her speeches on liberal values, in particular of equal opportunity for women, there is no record that she was herself formally affiliated with any suffrage organisation. Her friend Nora MacMunn (of whom more later) was a militant suffragette, and there is little doubt that the Williams' household at Cowley was feminist, but discretely so.

On 1 March 1907, the Bedfordshire Mercury reported on the Bedfordshire Temperance Society. From this, it seems that Ivy attended a committee meeting at which it was agreed that children in pubs were a bad idea –the meeting declaring, *"If England ever sank to be a 3rd or 4th rate power, it would be through the inebriety of the women of this country"*. There was a collection and the singing of hymns, and Ivy again addressed the assembly. She spoke of it being the eve of a great Temperance Reform with the tide changing, and again she spoke of the impact of 40 – 50 years of medical progress, of how in the past, in entertaining, wine would always be on the table but that

that was now no longer necessary and without it, one "*could still be a gentleman*". She declared that there was no need anymore to drink the King's health in wine. More pragmatically, she pointed out that Insurance policy charges were lower for abstainers. The report suggests a fairly impassioned speech. The arguments raised to reflect those at the time being expounded in America, where the prohibitionists were moving towards their goal of total prohibition attained in 1920. In England, there had been a strong Temperance movement in the nineteenth century amongst Christian groups leading in 1853 to the formation of the United Kingdom Alliance – a pressure group with the aim of persuading the government to introduce prohibition. The speeches Ivy made in support of this aim were part of this movement which led in 1914 to the Defence of the Realm Act, which first introduced limited pub licensing hours and the mandatory controls over the strength of the beer. Ironically the failure of prohibition as a movement in America discouraged the British Temperance movement, which disbanded in the 1930s.

On 9 March 1907, Ivy was elected president of the Oxford and District Sunday School Union; On 5 June 1907, the Oxford Times reported that Ivy had donated £10 and pledged the same amount going forward and regularly seems to have taken services for the Oxford Branch of the Railway Mission. This was also a Temperance society which had been founded in 1881; the Railway Mission aimed to improve the spiritual and physical wellbeing of railway workers. It soon joined the national battle against alcohol – the widespread mixture of drunkenness with the movement of heavy machinery was a fatal combination. The movement set up nearby coffee houses as an alternative to pubs. It built mission halls for prayer meetings, bible classes, evening lectures and vocational training and entertainment; the signature of pledge books was encouraged.

Ivy was at the time involved in land transactions acquiring land[21] and stood as one of the very many candidates for the Cowley Parish Council in 1907 and polled well, securing a seat.

On 16 March 1907, the Oxford Times reported on an address by Ivy to the George Street Congregational Sunday School (probably George Street Summertown, i.e. Middle Way). Ivy spoke at length on the influence of home life on children. She said that she wanted to speak to the mothers about the impact of the home. She anticipated as she had no children, she might be felt to have no right to speak, but she had been a child and had watched others' children. It was her belief that children also have an influence on the elders – and that home is the biggest influence – she then distributed prizes.

On 17 August 1907, the Oxford Times reported on the Oxford and District Sunday School Union's summer meeting at Witney, of which Ivy was President. There was an afternoon lecture in the Congregational chapel, which Ivy left early on account of indisposition. This is the first reference that I can find to an early bout of the chronic illness that seems to have beset Ivy in her early 30s. From

---

[21] Later that year she acquired land from Mr J Wheeler and James Batt (1908) – being two cottages

later references, it seems to me most likely that this was of a bronchial nature as she was, for example, urged to winter abroad. It still seems to have been troubling her in 1911 (although a bit improved), so it may have been a form of asthma or COPD. The activities Ivy undertook at around this time vary from the patronage of local church organisations and the parish to more politically driven work for the Liberal party or the Temperance movement – none of these seems directly to progress her wish to practice law. That she did not press this further may be a result of the ill health she suffered.

On 31 August 1907, The Oxford Journal reported on the Cowley parish council meeting held at Cowley Church. Ivy was by then a member (perhaps replacing her brother after his death and upon her removal to Cowley). The role she saw for herself was to understand and meet the needs of the community if need be from her own funds. The small record of this meeting is an interesting bit of light on the minutiae of the life she led at the time. It seems that at a previous meeting, the question of shelter, seating and swings in the recreational area had been considered and felt to be a good idea. Ivy had indicated a willingness to provide such seating at her own expense. At the subsequent meeting, Ivy repeated her offer to provide shelter and seats and swings for the ground but felt obliged to reduce her offer to 6 seats and 2 swings for reasons of the economy, although promising to do more the following year. That she was active in the community and not just a benefactor or speechmaker is apparent from her report of meetings she has had with the football and cricket club secretary to discuss their plans which at the time were too expensive. She also wanted to provide a district nurse for Cowley at the cost of £100 pa, of which she agreed to pay £70 on the proviso that it be a Queen's Nurse and work under an all –women committee (perhaps reflecting her personal experiences at the time). This may not only reflect her own poor health but of her promotion of women being active in the community. Her offer was accepted.

The next month on 7 September 1907, according to the Oxford Times, Ivy performed a stone laying in Long Hanborough for the new Sunday school in her capacity as President of the Oxford and District Sunday School Union. A couple of months later, in the same capacity, on 20 November 1907, she met district teachers at Wesley Hall, Cowley Road, where there were numerous companies represented and refreshments served. The attendees included the Rev Dr Arthur Staples of Beaver College USA (a women's seminary) and Rev W Cousins (her cousin and the famous missionary from Madagascar in the UK on leave), and H Liddell – the Son of Henry Liddell Oxford Don and headmaster of Westminster School. After the reception, the meeting adjourned to the chapel where Ivy presided. In reply, Rev Robertson said that Ivy occupied a place in their hearts for her "*warm sympathy*" for her interest in politics, temperance reform, and "*Sunday Schools.*"

1907 was a time of change for the women of England, and Oxford was no exception. Millicent Fawcett – leader of the women's suffrage movement – was to address the Oxford Union that year. The first Women's Social and Political Union ("WSPU") meeting was held in Oxford –

the WSPU had been formed in 1903 by the Pankhursts and extended its reach to the university at this time. Suffrage societies sprang up at Lady Margaret Hall and St Hugh's and in 1909 at St Hilda's. The Oxford Women Students' Society for Women's Suffrage was established in 1907. 1910 saw the Foundation of the Oxon, Berks, Bucks and Beds Federation of National Union of Women's Suffrage Societies.

However, it seems that Ivy was not to be part of this. In 1908 the Oxford Journal reported a further Cowley Parish council meeting. A letter of resignation from Ivy was read *"owing to continued ill –health"*. She regretted that she had been unable to do much for a long time but had kept hoping to get better. She sent good wishes and hoped to return one day. She did keep in contact with the council and, by 1911, was gratified to see a scheme instituted by her brother in 1902 to install street lighting in Cowley come to fruition and was credited at the meeting where the success of the scheme was announced, as being the first donor towards the cost of the scheme. In February 1909, she advertised for sale from the stables at Sunnyside, her valuable horse, saddlery and two carriages *"owing to the illness of owner and Physician's advice"*. Three years earlier, Charles Ewers had advertised for a second –hand wicker invalid chair; the time at which he started to assist Ivy is unknown and whilst it did occur to me that this might be the earliest sign of Ivy's ill health, the timing seems too early given the vigour with which she was campaigning in 1907 for Temperance measures. Her decline seems to have stemmed from 1907 and to have persisted until around 1911, necessitating not only rest but convalescing overseas.

There was at the same time a crisis within the wider Williams family. Harry Neville Prior, who had been a significant borrower from Ivy's father and who it seems had also borrowed from Adin Williams (and whose debt was forgiven in the will), finally found himself financially ruined. Harry Neville was universally liked and respected, and trusted by the Williams family – he looked after Eliza Williams after she was widowed and also looked after his own elderly father. He acted as executor of Adin and others. He was a hard worker. Family legend records a swindle that led to his downfall. He had entered into a partnership with his elder and more affluent brother in law, William Baker. That partnership was publicly severed, and whilst Harry Neville continued to try to run his own business, thereafter diversifying without success, in 1908, he was obliged to sell the large house he had built in Headington and remove to a much more modest property in Shotover. Ivy is inevitably bound to have been caught up in distress suffered by this. She had been a visitor to Highfield the house sold to meet the debts and indeed had counted it her home for a period whilst at the University. Throughout her life, she continued to keep a kindly eye on the Prior cousins and to employ Percy in due course as her solicitor. Whilst the world around her was changing, and women were becoming more vocal, Ivy faded from sight for a number of years, her health gradually improving, but spending much of her time overseas in an attempt to recover – most probably in Switzerland or the south of France. The references to presentations and speeches, to fetes and local meetings cease for this time, the few references to Ivy concerning donations she gives to the Radcliffe Hospital. Over the next few years (including the war years), she donated small amounts of money, mountains of eggs, dressing gowns, butter, crackers, cauliflowers, strawberries and cut flowers. In 1916 she became a "Life Governor" of the Radcliffe and paid a sum of £42 for the honour. Eventually, in 1922 when she moved from Sunnyside into a smaller, more central property, she was to give the entire estate to the hospital.

Business continued, however, to be transacted at King Edward Street, and the colourful mix of ideas and personalities of Oxford led in 1910 to the young Russian undergraduate Felix Yussapov living next door at 14 King Edward Street with two undergraduate friends, a Russian chef, a French Chauffeur, and English valet Arthur Keeping, a housekeeper and her husband who looked after his 3 horses –a hunter and two polo ponies. He also kept a bulldog and a macaw. This is the same Felix Yussapov who was subsequently linked to the assassination of Rasputin.

By 1911 the suffragette movement had boycotted the census; however, whilst Ivy's name is not to be found in the census of 1911, it is just as likely that she was recovering overseas as that she was deliberately refusing to participate. It was Ivy's style to argue and oppose but not to disobey. Ivy's home life and her relationship with her relatives were changing – Constance Cousins departed for India in 1911 at a time when Ivy's health was still fragile.

In 1913 the Great Pilgrimage to Hyde Park by Suffragettes took place, and acts of militancy started to be felt by suffragettes in London; Emily Wilding Davison drew attention to the cause by throwing herself under the feet of a Derby racehorse and dying. Emily Pankhurst was sentenced to three years in jail. The war was to change the role of women forever, and it was coming.

Chapter 7
The War 1914 –1918

During the war, there is little mention of Ivy. She seems to have been based mainly in Oxford and to have donated regularly to good causes, and to have changed her domestic servant. Her health seems to have improved. She returned to public service in a small way. Between 1916 –and 1919, she was treasurer of the Cowley War Savings Association[22], secretary to the parish council (1917 – 1918), librarian, and a member of the Cowley Emergency committee. On 11 July 1917, she was secretary of the executive committee of the Cowley branch of Oxfordshire County committee for War Savings, and in December 1917 was appointed secretary of the General Purposes Committee of Cowley War Distress Relief Fund[23]. Cowley had had a parish council only since 1894, and her brother Winter may have been a founder member. It was dissolved in 1929 and in spite of plans to create in its stead an independent Urban District Council, all matters of the council were, in fact, subsequently transferred to Oxford City. The various sub –committees

---

[22] This committee seems to have been the brain child of Ivy herself who, upon its being wound up in 1919 with the war savings certificates it had purchased being distributed to the members, was credited with the bulk of its achievements. It raised £4,500 pounds through collections and was staffed by the parish council.

[23] As well as working for this committee – again primarily a fund-raising body but also one that managed practical problems such as finding employment, both Ivy and her mother were financial contributors to this fund.

established locally and in which Ivy participated were features of Oxford in wartime, concentrating on financial stability and relief of poverty. Parish councils were (and still are) often the supervisors of allotments and charities, and Cowley was no different, so an infrastructure within the parish council was already in place to ensure that locally there was support for the impact of war. As well as the need to raise funds, these councils were also concerned with on the ground problems such as finding accommodation for Belgian refugees. There is no record of Ivy providing practical assistance with this, although she and her mother lived in a substantial property which was in due course used as an institution, so it may well be that she did offer accommodation.

It can be assumed that she was at this time returned to good health. She was also able to offer remote tutoring in Italian to Home –Students and worked May 1918 –Feb 1919 at Thomas Mallam's law office. Mallam had been a parish councillor with her in Cowley and would have been well aware of her abilities.

The solicitors' offices stood at 126, High Street, not far from Adin Williams' first foothold in Oxford. The building still stands; the cellars are said to date from the 13th century. Like the Williams family home on the High street, the building had operated both as a place of business and home. The original trade was the sale of tobacco; however, from the end of the 18th century, the family diversified into auctioneering and land agency. The solicitor's firm was started in 1830, marking the end of the tobacco trade. A member of the Mallam family continued to have a direct involvement until about 1940.

A law firm still operates from the premises. In 1918 the firm was likely to have concentrated mainly on land transactions, an area where Ivy had significant expertise, which she was to display at her Bar finals in the next few years.

War changed Oxford forever. It transformed itself from a fairly inward –looking place of academic excellence to an international City host to refugees from Serbia and Belgium and a major hospital centre. The number of male students plummeted as the young answered the call to arms. Women's numbers, on the contrary, rose steadily. Women were encouraged to complete their studies as there would be a need for teachers and other educated people after the war ended. Somerville College was requisitioned as a hospital as it was situated adjacent to the Radcliffe, and a physical connection was established. Somerville ladies were relocated to a discrete area in Oriel College.

There was an egg collection scheme in place throughout the war, which may explain why Ivy was so diligent in her donations of eggs. Sunnyside, at the time, stood on a plot of 50 acres of land and had agricultural units – piggeries, gardens, paddocks. It was undoubtedly used as a food production unit and, in due course, was itself to serve as a convalescent hospital after the war.

Ivy's family was directly touched by the war. Of her cousins, at least two volunteered, Rex and Robin Prior being deployed to France, where Rex was to die (he is commemorated at Headington Quarry church where his father is buried), and Robin was injured in May 1917. Ivy looked after the Prior family in later years, and although

Robin had already moved away from Oxford when he was injured, Rex was the baby of the family, and his death hit his mother hard. She died in 1920. Rex is buried in Doullens in the Somme. The family paid to ensure that his gravestone contained personal details of his life.

Business continued during the war. As a trustee of her father's trust fund, Ivy sold the Electra Palace (a cinema) in 1917, starting the liquidation of his large real estate portfolio.

The war was followed by a period of financial hardship and the misery of Spanish flu, which devastated predominantly the young of the nation between 1918 and 1920. In recognition of the war work done by women and the need for their continued involvement, the Representation of the People Act of 1918 finally gave the vote to women over the age of 30.

Chapter 8
Academia

From about 1920, Ivy's focus seems to have turned firmly to the University. She had retained contact with her old college and, through the war years, had offered some distance tutoring in Italian. How she came to be appointed as a law tutor by the Society of Oxford Home –Students is unknown. There is no record of an application by her, but she was by 1920 a distinguished local figure and had had direct legal experience in local solicitor's offices. It is also the case that at the time there were relatively few women law students at the college, so the job was fairly small in terms of tutoring, although she seems immediately to have taken a keen interest in the research potential of the role. Probably by mutual agreement in1920, Ivy Williams became the tutor in Jurisprudence to the Society of Oxford Home –Students and Oxford's (and England's) first woman teacher of the law. She was at the time undertaking a significant restructuring of her life and finances and was bent on local philanthropy. Her move to Staverton Road – to the house she called "Cote" after her grandfather's origins were imminent. She was still based at Sunnyside in 1919 as her mother made her will that year and gave her address as Sunnyside. By 1921 mother and daughter had moved to Staverton Road, and "Sunnyside Homes" had come into existence (in fact, these may have predated the move suggesting that Ivy divested herself of part or all of the Sunnyside estate prior to her move).

In February 1919, The Barristers and Solicitors Bill was introduced to allow women into the profession, something that Ivy will have followed closely, its passage through Parliament was ended by the wider provisions of the Sex Disqualification (Removal) Act of 1919, which came into effect on 23 December 1919. Accordingly, whilst accepting a role at the Society of Home –Students, Ivy's foremost attention was on the possibility now opening before her of a call to the Bar. Her contemporary Helena Normanton joined Middle Temple on 24th December 1919. Ivy applied to Inner Temple shortly after.

Meanwhile, however, Ivy was drawn into academic life. A talented linguist (her subsequent public appointments owed much to her language skills), Ivy was also at this time engaged in co –editing a translation from Russian and, at the age of 42 in 1920 collaborated with the mercurial Nevill Forbes (a Slavonic scholar) to publish an introduction, notes and vocabulary on a collection of four short stories by Russian author VM Garshin.

Cementing the appointment by the Society of Home – Students, Ivy was one of the large cohorts of women at the first –degree ceremony on 14 October 1920, where her successive examination achievement resulted in her being awarded a BA in Jurisprudence, an MA and a BCL. The picture below (for which I am indebted to St Anne's) is of a later gathering of women that year to celebrate their degrees.

Photo supplied courtesy of St Anne's College Oxford

Ivy was also at this time taking steps to further endow the Congregational church by passing them the property at All Hallows, which had become the Manse. It seems to have housed the ministers for the church and to have been owned by the Williams family. In all likelihood, this is the property that Winter Williams had lived in (and died in), which had reverted to Ivy on his intestacy, and been redeployed for this purpose at that time. Emma Williams' will, made in 1919, left a sum for the upkeep of the Manse. Ivy eventually transferred the property to the church in 1924.

From the outset of her time at the Home –Students, Ivy seems to have formed a good working relationship with Professor Geldart.

On her appointment in 1920, Ivy set about identifying a topic for her Oxford doctorship. For this, she was advised by Professor William Martin Geldart (1870 –1922).

William Geldart was a leading jurist of his time and had been the Vinerian Professor of English law at Oxford. He was also a member of the Hebdomadal Council[24] in 1905 and chaired the University's Delegacy for Women Students 1911 –1921 (where after it was dissolved). His advice to Ivy in 1920 was to undertake research into the Swiss Code of 1907 not only as an interesting subject but also as one that had had little published on it in England. Ivy divided her work into a descriptive analysis of the sources with a view to subsequently providing an English translation of the trilingual Code (something that she eventually did in 1925). Ivy acknowledged Professor Geldart, who died before her first work was published and indeed before she was called to the Bar (he died in a sanatorium in Jamaica after a brief illness aged only 51 in 1922, although he had previously described himself as a retired law tutor) in her Preface as " *a loss to the legal world at large and to the women students at Oxford [who will be deeply mourned]* ".

After the death of Geldart's wife Emily in 1937 Ivy personally commissioned a plaque for Professor Geldart in 1938, and St Anne's book of Benefactors for 1938 reads "*1938. Ivy Williams. Tablet in the Geldart Library to commemorate the benefaction of Professor Geldart, designed by Sir Giles Gilbert Smith.*"

Like Ivy, Geldart was a talented linguist. He is much revered by St Anne's College, which has named its library and law society after him.

---

[24] The executive council for the management of Oxford University.

Bertha Johnson, the redoubtable principal of the Society of Oxford Home –Students, retired very shortly after Ivy's appointment as law tutor to the college. In 1921 she was presented with a volume to mark her retirement, which included signed photographs of some of her former students.

Photo courtesy of St Anne's College Oxford. This is almost contemporaneous with the photo of Ivy at the 1920 graduation gathering above.

It is interesting to note the changes in Ivy's appearance in the two photos from her earlier pictures. The picture above shows Ivy in a reflective mood, the customary thin –rimmed glasses worn constantly, her hair originally fair now darkened and as always tied back. It is unexpected to see her wearing a cardigan over a crisp and decorative white blouse. Surprisingly the cardigan seems to have seen better days. She seems to have lost weight since her student days. The group photo on the previous page is powerful and iconic. The intelligent faces of a fairly mature group of women new graduates face the camera defiantly. They flank their principal, who is majestic in the forefront, with her cane. Ivey stands to the left of Mrs Johnson, facing away from the camera.

Ivy's "Sources of the Law in the Swiss Civil Code" was completed by her in 1922 and published in 1923 by the Oxford University Press. In 1976 a further edition was published. It is still available today.

Chapter 9
The Race to the Bar

That Ivy became the first woman to be called to the English Bar when Inner Temple called her in May 1922 is now history. That she was able to leap –frog other women contenders due to her academic excellence is also well known. What is not so well known is that just at the time when obstacles were removed from her progress, clearing the way for her to fulfil her father's dream for her, her mother (with whom she had lived since her father's death) died.

With the enactment of the Sex Disqualification Act at the age of 42 in January 1920, Ivy Williams enrolled as a student at the Bar and was admitted to Inner Temple. Her sponsor for her call was Sir John Simon (1873 –1954). Sir John was the highest –paid barrister of his time and a Liberal politician. In choosing him, Ivy was taking no chances. He was to become Lord Chancellor in his time and was very "connected". He was the son of a Congregational minister, which I had thought might explain why Ivy was able to enlist him as a sponsor; however, he was an atheist, so his position as a fellow of All Souls and Liberal politician might better explain the connection. Winter Williams had been promoted by a fellow at All Souls – H. Duff, who had contacted Frederick Pollock (1845 –1937) on his behalf to be his sponsor – Pollock was a barrister and Oxford tutor at the time of Winter's application and had been professor of common law at the Inns of Court until 1890. As treasurer of Lincoln's Inn, it is unclear why he was approached to sponsor a barrister joining Inner Temple.

In the Easter term (Trinity) that year, Ivy passed the first tranche of Bar exams. On 1st July 1920, the Church Militant congratulated her on her first in Constitutional Law and Legal History. In the Christmas term (Michaelmas), she sat the second tranche getting a first in Conveyancing (perhaps drawing on her experience at Mallams during the war). Whilst she obtained the best marks on that paper, she had already said that she did not intend to practice. Overall, she came second out of 123 candidates.

The 1921 Census shows Ivy and her mother Emma based at 28, Nassington Road in Hampstead – Ivy is described as a tutor and lecturer at Oxford but working "from home", Emma as a widow with domestic duties; there is no other person at the house suggesting that they did not keep a servant. It is likely that Ivy had taken a leave of absence from light tutoring duties at the Society of Home – Students and was at the time studying for her final Bar exams and to complete the dining requirements of the Bar – she completed ten terms of dining. She had engaged the services of Mr Cuthbert Spurling, formerly of Christchurch Oxford as a tutor (and later described him as a marvel of clarity) – Mr Spurling had chambers in London and was a professional tutor to the Bar. He had obtained a first in History at Oxford and a 2nd in Civil law and wrote a manual of Common Law for practitioners and students in 1898. His occupation in the 1911 census is given as barrister and Bar coach. He was particularly successful as a tutor to the Bar (at a time when not all students employed tutors) – for example, in Ivy's year, he coached both her and the only other student awarded a first in the Bar finals.

In the middle of her studies (and tragically before seeing Ivy called), on 8 July 1921, Ivy's mother died in Nassington Road and was buried in Highgate cemetery. Her grave stands alone. It is difficult to understand why she was not buried with her husband in Oxford. It is marked by a substantial pink granite headstone common at the time and highly durable. Emma Ewers was buried 10 feet deep. This suggests – as does the significant space left on the headstone – that provision was being made in 1921 for at least one and quite possibly more burials in the grave. Whether Ivy was simply being practical and had in mind perhaps her own burial or whether perhaps was creating a family plot is impossible to say. In her own will, Ivy left instructions for the upkeep of her mother's grave (which have sadly not been actioned; however, the grave is in good condition owing to the durability of the material chosen for the headstone) but chose to be cremated quietly.

Emma left a short Will. It is dated 3rd March 1919, at which time Emma was living at Sunnyside. The grant of probate makes it clear that whilst at the time of death she resided at 30 Staverton Road, she was formerly of Sunnyside and also of 28 Nassington Road, Hampstead, where she died.

The will is a tour de force of feminism; it provides for the appointment of Ivy as sole executrix and trustee; it gives £50 to her housekeeper Miss Jackson (who continued to assist Ivy after her mother's death), and £50 to Lizzie

Horn of Summertown (the same Lizzie Horn that her late husband had left a bequest to for her help with his mother – Emma seems to have had a more informal relationship with her than George had). She gave £100 to her sister (Rosa Ewers) and to each of her sisters in law (at the time of her death, there were probably 4 living) and to her natural nieces (probably about 13 living at the time of Emma's death) and to Miss Emily Prior. Emily Prior was herself a formidable lady (she was the intellectual sister of Harry Neville Prior). She then left £50 to her nephew's wives (3 in number) and £25 to every female child of her nephews and nieces (numbering more than 15).

This left £100 for at least 13 natural nieces (£1300);

£100 to 5 sisters or sisters in law and also to Emily Prior (£600);

At least 3 bequests of £50 to nephew's wives (£150);

And at least 15 bequests of £25 to every female child of her nieces and nephews (which included my mother) (£375);

She left £100 in trust for the upkeep of Sunny Side Homes and £100 for the trust for the upkeep of Cowley Manse. She left all her personal effects to Ivy except "[her] keeper," which she left to her niece Ada Cousins, who was the unmarried daughter of William Cousins, who looked after the family home at Chalfont Road.

The residue of her estate was left to her sister Rosa Ewers. It was witnessed by William Cousins at his home at 11 Chalfont Road and by Mabel Olive Rose at the Manse in Cowley. In short, Emma left at least 36 individual bequests to family members, all of whom were female. No male relative or friend received a penny.

There was no financial need to leave anything to Ivy, who had benefitted from her father's will, which enabled her to look after her mother.

Probate was granted to Ivy on 3rd September 1921; the gross value of the estate was £3,893 –7 –6; net £3,846 –6 –6 (approximately £200,000 in 2021 terms) (more than half of which was consumed by individual gifts).

Towards the end of 1921, in November, the Oxford Chronicle and Reading Gazette picked up the results of the Bar finals, identifying Ivy as the senior student and candidate with the highest marks. In spite of this, it is also noted that Ivy had no intention of practicing herself. In her finals in October 1921 at the Council for Legal Education, Ivy became the first woman to get a first[25]; there were 123 candidates, including 12 women – of which there were 99 "passes", 30 –second classes and only 2 "firsts". The other first was Mr H F Dunkley of Cambridge, also (like Ivy) tutored by Cuthbert Spurling. Ivy was quoted by the Oxford Chronicle as stating that whilst she herself would not practice that she would prepare girls for the exams and that *"they will practice"*. As she got a first, there was a discretion to advance her, which was exercised by excusing her certain dining requirements. In her interview, she explained that for women lawyers, she saw women and children as natural clients but also saw a need for slow progress. When asked,

---

[25] In this she was not the first woman to pass the Bar – that honour fell to Olive Clapham

she opined that there would be women judges but *"not for a very long time"* simply because very few barristers were elevated to the bench. She was asked if she thought that there should be separate courts for women but thought that unnecessary.

Ivy managed to get herself to the front of the several women eager to be called to the Bar by virtue of excellent exam results. However, she might have had to share that honour with Gwyneth Bebb but for a tragic event. Gwyneth Bebb and other women had, in 1912, sued the Law Society to allow them to sit the solicitors' exams. Their applications were refused by the Law Society, and the group decided to test the decision by appealing to the courts. In this, they were represented by leading counsel. Their application was famously rejected initially by the same judge that had rebuffed Bertha Cave and ultimately by the Court of Appeal. Reading the judgment of the Court of Appeal with twenty –first –century eyes, it is hard to understand the logic and motivation behind the findings. To intellectual women of the era, it must have been frustrating in the extreme. The basis of the judgement was that as women had never been lawyers, there was no precedent for them ever becoming lawyers, they being under a common law disability and not qualifying as "persons" and as such disentitled from practicing. Feeling ran high amongst the more liberal members of the legal profession, and various Bills[26] were proposed to Parliament to redress the position that was felt by many to be intolerable in post –war Britain.

---

[26] E.g. 1913 The Legal Profession (Admission of Women) Bill and Barristers and Solicitors (Qualification of Women) Bill 1919.

In the intervening period after her case was dismissed and prior to the passing of legislation to redress the position Gwyneth Bebb, who had studied law at Oxford at St Hugh's College in 1908 –1911, obtaining a first –class degree mark, became a political and feminist activist. She was amongst the first tranche of women allowed to graduate in 1920 at Oxford and the only one of them to hold a first –class degree. She had married a solicitor and had been appointed as an assistant commissioner for the enforcement for the ministry of Food – work that included prosecution of black marketeers. She applied to Lincoln's Inn to be admitted as a student barrister in 1918 without success. With the passing of the Sex Disqualification (Removal) Act 1919, she immediately reapplied and was admitted as a student on 27 January 1920. Later that year, she resigned from her job to concentrate on studying for the Bar exams and to continue to assist her husband in his legal practice. Whether Bebb would have matched or exceeded Ivy in the final exams will never be known as Bebb gave birth to her second daughter in August 1921, and both mother and baby were to die of complications that Autumn.

In April 1922, the press noted that Ivy was to be called in May as the only female barrister of the intake. It reported her dining obligations, although only partially completed, would be prematurely brought to an end as she had been granted the certificate of honour (a discretionary release from the formality for excellence in the exams) by the Inn. In the run –up to that event, the newspapers speculated much on what she would wear.

And so, it was that on 10th May1922 Ivy Williams, aged 44, *"The daughter of George St. Swithin Williams late of 12, King Edward Street, Oxford, solicitor. Miss Williams belongs to an old Oxford family"* was called to Bar by Inner Temple marking the end of the struggle for equality in the legal profession and opening the door to many other younger women set on a legal career. The press reported that she made an emotional but modest speech in slow, deliberate tones and had been granted permission to drink water and did not wear a wig. The Daily Herald ran a picture of Ivy ("Miss Ivy Williams BCL MA") and reported that she wore a black evening dress, student gown and bands. In her speech, Ivy referred to the fact that her call *"had been her and her father's dream"*, but that for her personally, it had come too late, and she spoke instead of those who will come after.

The senior bencher who administered the call was Charles Dickens' son Henry Fielding Dickens. He was at pains in describing the progress of women *"from chattel to barrister"* to attribute their progress not to militancy but to their war effort. To mark the occasion, he presented Ivy with a copy of "David Copperfield", which St Anne's College retained in their library. His speech is perhaps disappointing as there had been the opportunity to right the wrong of the failed worthy candidates of the previous decades rather than to give the impression that it was only more recently that women had somehow "earned" the right to join a profession that had done all it could to resist them.

132

Chapter 10
Scholarship and illness

At the time of the call and following the death of her mother, Ivy completed a substantial reorganisation of her personal affairs. She finalised the transfer of Sunnyside and its grounds to the Radcliffe infirmary and also disposed of the Manse at All Hallows to the Congregational Church, valued at £650, completing all formalities in 1923. She also continued her academic work on the Swiss Code.

On 2 June 1922, Vote National Executive met and passed a special resolution of warm congratulations to Ivy and expressed indignation at the rejection of Lady Rhondda's appeal to sit in the House of Lords[27]. Ivy's contemporary, the Indian lady lawyer Dr Cornelia Sorabji was at this

---

[27] This was a reference to Margaret Haig Thomas, 2nd Viscountess Rhondda. She was the daughter of a suffragette and went to Somerville but left after 2 terms. She worked for her father in Cardiff docks, married a local landowner and joined the Women's Social and Political Union and was secretary of the Newport branch. She campaigned often in hostile conditions and was an extremist, attending protest marches with Pankhursts, and jumping onto Asquiff's running board, attempting to destroy a post box with a chemical bomb. She was sent to jail but was released as she went on hunger strike. She abandoned suffrage during the war and worked with father in US to arrange supplies to UK forces, but became depressed with her marriage failing. She was on the Lusitania when it was torpedoed; her father and secretary made it to lifeboats but she did not and was eventually rescued from a piece of board suffering from hypothermia from which she took a long time to recover. On the death of her father she was awarded the Viscountess title by special remainder but was regularly frustrated in attempts to take her seat. Only after her death was this allowed. She set up the Six Point Group. After her divorce she preferred to live with women including Vera Brittain's friend Winifred Holtby

time starting her extensive work with the women of India who lacked representation.

As part of the reorganisation of her affairs following the death of her mother on 2 February 1923 the Westminster Gazette reported that the convocation of Oxford would be asked the next Tuesday to accept an offer from Ivy Williams of the Society of Home –Students of two sums of £3,500 each for 2 scholarships in jurisprudence in memory of Winter Williams. One was to have an annual value of £80, and one was to be for women only. The scholarship fund was invested prudently by the university and still exists today to help students of the law. Now known as the Winter Williams Studentship and worth £7,500 pa, it can be awarded for any one of the law faculty's graduate degrees.

On 17 November 1923, Percy Prior recorded in his letters book writing to his cousin Henry Williams in Canada

> "*My father [Harry Neville Prior] and I were present this afternoon at the ceremony granting the degree of Doctor of Civil Law at Oxford to my cousin Ivy. She is the only woman to hold that Degree, except for those few on whom it has been conferred "honoris causa" – honorary, without any examinations. Wouldn't it have been a triumph for her father had he been alive to see it?*"

Ivy's health had always been a serious concern to her. It had caused her to resign from her work at Cowley Parish council in her younger years and to give up riding and driving on doctor's orders. At some stage in late 1923 or early 1924, she was working at Lac Leman in Lausanne on her translation of the Swiss Legal code when she indulged in skiing in Switzerland. This is likely to have been cross country skiing, as downhill was at the time in its infancy. From reading my cousin's legal work and thinking about her list of good works and sober lifestyle, I had come to think of her as somewhat prim and retiring; I am almost certainly doing her a disservice in this as her early interview with the Oxford newspapers suggested that she was an accomplished sportswoman and so it's perhaps not surprising that she took the opportunity to try out winter sports when in residence in Switzerland at a fairly advanced age.

She seems to have suffered what was thought at the time to have been a minor knee injury. It was, however, to trouble her for the rest of her life.

Her cousin Percy reported on 24 February 1924 that she had been admitted to the private Headington Orthopaedic Hospital as the injury from the skiing accident to her knee had got worse.

In June 1924, she underwent a further operation on her knee in Oxford, and by the first of September 1924, she was still in hospital, making (according to Percy) "*very slow progress*". Her convalescence continued for a period of four years, although she was able in 1925 to publish a three –volume translation of the trilingual Swiss Civil Code. Those of my family who remember her recall that she always walked with a limp.

In 1926, her uncle Charles, who had been her financial advisor, died, and Ivy arranged for the collection of papers he held for her at 12, King Edward Street (which she continued to own and which seems to have operated as offices for various businesses after her father's death until 1927 when it was sold for £918) including Winter's papers. These she sent to storage to Miss Jackson in "Cote". When I first read this entry in Percy Prior's letter book, I assumed that the family retained property in Cote and that her mother's helper Miss Jackson also lived there. In fact, on further reflection, I am fairly sure that the property referred to is Ivy's house on Staverton Road, where at various times Miss Jackson provided housekeeping and nursing services to both Emma Williams and to Ivy. In early correspondence, the property is named "Cote".

After Charles' death in 1926, Ivy asked her cousin Percy Prior – a solicitor and conveyancing specialist –to handle her affairs following the death of Charles. At the time, she was continuing her convalescence in Harrogate at Stray Sea nursing home Victoria Avenue doing sea swimming for therapy; she moved to 13, York Place Harrogate a little later. Letters from Percy report that she had a tricycle and was gaining weight (a good thing). On 5 October 1926, she had her tonsils removed in Harrogate.

In 1927 she had a relapse that found her once again in a nursing home in July, although she continued to liquidate and distribute her estate. As well as selling the house at King Edward Street, she collected various ground rents and sold the property she held in Sunderland. The clearance of King Edward Street was done for her by Charles' daughter Florence (who seems to have been of a nervous disposition) and Percy, and as well as generating a lot of paperwork also led to the rediscovery of Winter's typewriter which Percy appropriated. The next year saw full voting rights for women (previously restricted to the older age group).

In spite of a period of relative inactivity, Ivy was mentioned in February 1928 in Weekly Despatch London *"where women can score"* in an article by Ann Gray, which contained a picture of Ivy at her call and the observation that, in her opinion, it would take 15 years minimum call before women become judges – this was not a particularly controversial statement as that period of time was the average for all barristers.

By September 1928, Ivy was again in a nursing home, this time in Wales. She was, however, busy and active in managing her affairs. She wrote to Percy that she wanted to send £12 –10 to uncle Horace Williams in Ontario as a present, having heard (somehow) that he was hard up. She was still experiencing problems with her knee. After her stay in Wales, it seems that her health had improved sufficiently for her to resume a fairly active life. However, a further tragedy befell her. In 1929 Nevill Forbes died. Nevill was a tutor in Russian at Oxford, and when she had first been appointed to the Society of Home –Students, Ivy had collaborated with him on a translation with notes of a work of Garshin. Outside of her work on the Swiss Code, this is the only academic work credited to her, and it preceded her legal work. Nevill was her first sponsor and colleague at Oxford and was clearly of importance to her. He was a controversial figure, being openly gay at a time when homosexuality was illegal. He was also of a nervous disposition and, like Ivy, had great concerns for his health. His cause of death was suicide.

Chapter 11
Representing British women at the Hague Conference 1930

In 1930 a Conference was held at the Hague between March 13 and April 12, optimistically seeking the codification of International Law in three areas. It was attended by representatives of 47 governments and one observer (the USSR). This was the first such conference of its type, although in 1924, The League of Nations had set up a Committee of Experts for the progressive codification of International law. That committee proposed certain areas of law for consideration by the conference in the hope of achieving some sort of consistency internationally. The 1930 conference elected to consider three areas of law with an International dimension—Nationality, Territorial Waters and The Responsibility of States for Damage caused in their Territory to the Person or Property of Foreigners.

In preparation for the conference, a five –man Preparatory Committee was established, which drew up and disseminated quite elaborate questionnaires on each of the three areas to participating governments. A lot of paperwork was generated in reply. From that database, the Preparatory committee then drew up a series of "Bases" on points raised in each of the subjects. From these "bases", each country selected its delegates with specific reference to the topics under discussion.

Ultimately the British delegation consisted of 3 male delegates and 5 technical delegates, of whom Ivy was the only woman, and a male secretary. Australia adopted the exact same delegates to represent them. The Great Britain and Northern Ireland "team" was led by academic and judge Sir Maurice Gwyer (1978 –1952), later to be a judge in India and benefactor to the university in Delhi. At the time he was the Treasury Solicitor. Mr Oscar Follett Dowson OBE (later Sir Oscar) (1879 –1961) was an assistant legal adviser to the Home Office, later to be the chief advisor. His military and naval background gave him an interest in the Territorial waters' debates, although he is chiefly remembered for his works on election law. The third team member was William Eric Beckett, KCMG QC (1896 –1966), legal advisor to the foreign office. He also seems to have been primarily interested in the territorial waters question and to have had pragmatic skills (which were ignored by the conference, which failed to reach an agreement). The team were assisted by five technical advisors, a Mr A.W Brown LLD, solicitor to the treasury; Mr W.H Hancock, Secretary to the Navy; Mr G. S. King MC solicitor to the government; Lieutenant Commander R M Southern, a hydrographic officer in the Navy and Miss Ivy Williams DCL LLD.

There was some controversy in the selection of a woman in the British delegation. Many countries had none – indeed, of the hundreds of delegates, only 8 were women. Ivy was the "safe" choice of the British government, seen as unlikely to "rock the boat". She was not, however, the first choice. That fell to Chrystal Macmillan (1872 – 1937), a feminist lawyer. Chrystal was a graduate of Edinburgh University and was called to the Bar by Middle Temple in 1924 after completion of war duties for the peace movement.

She was from a large wealthy family and had been amongst the first tranche of female science graduates of

Edinburgh University. She went on to complete a Masters in mental and moral philosophy and then the law. In1908, she was the first female advocate to appear before the House of Lords when as a litigant in person, she attempted to gain voting rights for women in university seats, which failed. She had campaigned against the legal requirement for women to lose their UK citizenship when marrying a foreign national. She was secretary of the International Woman Suffrage alliance from 1913 –to 1920 and had a role in organising the International Congress of Women in the Hague in 1915 to try to end war. She had also been a participant in the International Congress of Women in Zurich in May 1919 and then appointed delegate for that congress to the Paris Peace Conference. She stood as an unsuccessful Liberal Candidate in 1935.

Chrystal turned down the invitation to be a delegate to the Hague Conference in spite of significant experience with such conferences and well –known expertise on the thorny question of women's nationality when married to a foreigner, which had been thrown into sharp focus by her experiences during the war. Her reason was that she did not wish to be constrained by the "party line" of the UK Government.

On 4 April 1930, Vote recorded that the Women's Freedom League had declined to nominate anyone until the UK government position was made clear – it then chose Ivy

Earlier, at the end of January 1930, "Common Cause" reported on the pending delegation to the Conference at the Hague. The government had asked for suggestions for a woman to go to The Hague. In response, the NUSEC put forward Ivy as well suited, although her views did not entirely coincide with those of the women's organisations. As a technical delegate, Ivy would be bound by government rules, and as a balance, the NUSEC suggested that a free unattached assessor, namely Chrystal Macmillan, be included in the delegation. Chrystal was a more radical choice – although Ivy was a member of the British Federation of University Women ("BFUW") and indeed chaired a subcommittee on the question of the nationality of married women. The BFUW had lobbied the Home Secretary to include a woman in the delegation. With the subsequent withdrawal of Chrystal on ideological grounds, Ivy's pre –eminence as a barrister, Oxford lecturer, and her international law expertise (based largely on her work on the Swiss Code and also on the tutelage of the then Oxford Professor of International Law – James Brierly who was a member of the preparatory committee that paved the way for the Conference) led to her nomination by the BFUW. Ivy was very interested in the task and wrote regularly requesting details of progress with her appointment. The Sheffield Daily Telegraph, in reporting her selection as a delegate on 5 Feb 1930, recorded that she was the choice of the National Union of Societies for Equal Citizenship. The NUSEC was the successor organisation to the National Union of Women's Suffrage Society, founded in 1897 and of which it is assumed Ivy was a member. This union was not of a militant tendency.

Chrystal had published various works about the nationality of married women prior to the conference. She held, however, firm views from which she would not diverge. She clashed directly with Ivy in the run –up to the conference. The clash was one of principle versus pragmatism. Ivy corresponded with a colleague Sybil Campbell[28] complaining that she feared that Chrystal's

---

[28] Sybil was the first woman to be appointed a stipendiary magistrate in England in 1954; prior to that she had been called to the Bar by Middle Temple shortly after Ivy's own call.

insistence on equality would defeat a pragmatic compromise (on which Ivy was proved correct).

She wrote: –

"[Chrystal] still puts the principle of equality first, whereas I have been saying that we should consider ourselves first as lawyers who would help to forward international agreement and only secondarily as women".

Chrystal became a member of the subcommittee chaired by Ivy at the BFUW, which led to a sometimes heated exchange of correspondence as each defended their own position

Broadly there were two approaches to the question of the nationality of women after marriage to a foreigner. There were those countries (the majority –following the approach of the French) who thought that the woman (and any children) should in marriage "transfer" to the nationality of the husband irrevocably (to promote "family unity"), and there were those that considered that the parties to the marriage should each be entitled to retain their own nationality. The issue had been thrown into sharp focus for women after the First World War, where some women had found themselves classified as enemy aliens and even stateless. Chrystal put equality first and last in all her dealings and was a steadfast suffragist. She was clear that if the UK Government required a more nuanced approach, she could not deliver. She also took some exception to the fact that the appointment was to be as a "technical advisor" to the delegation, which meant that she would only be entitled to point out matters to the committee and not to make specific recommendations.

In announcing her selection as the British delegate, full weight was given to Ivy's qualifications – DCL (Ox), LLD (Lon) and Barrister of Inner Temple, plus her excellence as a linguist and student of foreign systems abroad. Common Cause observed that the British Government favoured the principle that a British woman who marries an alien should not lose her nationality without her consent.

Ivy was to meet the other leading female lawyers of her time at The Hague.

These included: –

Miss Emma Wold (1871 –1950) – an American suffragist, president of College Equal Suffrage association Oregon, also from Washington Law School, a promotor of Black rights with a special interest in women's nationality if marrying a foreigner. She was appointed by Hoover to the Hague.

Mlle Marcelle Renson (1894 –1988) – a militant Belgian feminist and one of the first Belgian female barristers

Dr Marie Luders (1878 –1966) was a politician and women's rights activist, one of the first women to go to university in Germany – she had been arrested and imprisoned by Gestapo; she was responsible for Lex Luders, a law governing the rights of foreigners married to Germans

Mrs Schonfeld Polano -Dutch

Dr Krlova – Horakova – Czech

It seems that there were 8 women delegates,

and of these, 5 were also members of FIFU[29] (i.e. Ivy, Marie Luders, Kathleen Phelan (Irish barrister at Law), Anka Godjevac and Marcelle Renson)

On 4 April 1930, International Women's suffrage News proclaimed in French that

---

[29] Federation Internationale des femmes Universitaires

"L'Union National welcomes the nomination of Ivy Williams as a technical delegate to the Codification conference of the Hague".

Predictably the conference failed to find unity on the question of how nationality should be determined. Ivy spoke once at a meeting of the Nationality Subcommittee – using her linguistic skills, she spoke in French, which was the language of the majority of those in attendance. She reminded the committee of certain principles that she felt they should give weight to.

"The main difficulty is the need for family unity. Suitable legislative provision could be made for this, however; the difficulty is by no means insuperable. Does anyone seriously believe that, by obliging a woman to change her nationality, family accord is made more secure? Can it be argued that, if the woman is allowed to choose her nationality, such family concord will be diminished?

No, gentlemen. The woman would always sacrifice herself for her husband and her children; this has always been the case through history. We have no right to assume that a woman's' first thought would not be for her family. She would certainly consider her family's interests and make her choice accordingly"

It is not immediately apparent from this where Ivy's sympathies lay. On the one hand, she is speaking against the automatic selection of the husband's nationality for the woman upon marriage but on the other, suggesting that it is likely to happen in any event due to human nature. Later in her speech, she did make reference to the principle of equality and the practical consequences of a woman being forced to accept an alien nationality on, for example, employment rights, especially in the case of

144

depression. The approach is a strange mix of a slightly rose –tinted (and theoretical) view of the way in which a marriage should work, based perhaps on her own happy childhood, and a non –interventionalist view on domestic laws.

This is not the only example of Ivy the spinster pontificating on how families operate. At local Sunday School meetings back in Oxford, she was used to recommending how children should be bought up (she explained her qualifications for taking upon herself such advice as being the fact that she had herself once been a child).

With the failure of the Hague Conference to agree on any generally acceptable codification of law as regards the nationality of women and children, Chrystal Macmillan organised an International Committee for Action on the Nationality of Married Women the following year. She gained support from several women's groups supporting the working woman. They hoped to delay the Hague Conference by publishing a watered –down codification that did not give women equal rights with men; in this, they were successful in lobbying the League of Nations, but in spite of study groups being established, these were unable to agree on basic principles of equality. Perhaps inevitably, the failure to agree led to the League of Nations disregarding the work done by the woman's groups, and 7 years later, the Hague Convention was ratified.

Ivy was a supporter of the British Commonwealth League, which held annual conferences on matters of particular significance to women, which conferences were attended by members of women's suffrage societies from around the world. Almost all speakers were women, and the areas covered were wide –ranging and comprehensively considered from the standpoint of the various countries most particularly affected. For example, in 1930, at the conference held in June, shortly after her return from the Hague, she interjected in respect of a proposed resolution to be put to further conferences (Colonial and Imperial Conferences) concerning the position of women working as prostitutes and the provision of free medical aid. Ivy requested an amendment to the resolution to the effect that free and secret treatment should be available to all suffering from venereal diseases. The amendment she suggested was withdrawn upon a slight reduction in the scope of the original resolution. To me, this shows a mind very invested in the minutiae of conference materials and at the same time, in spite of the fairly prim impression, one may have of a teetotaller spinster, a degree of open – mindedness.

Advertising material for the 1931 Conference included reference to the fact that Ivy would be speaking and Ivy continued to be interested in women's rights with an international dimension. At the next conference, she delivered a paper on the Law of Inheritance in England and the Dominions and its bearing on women. This is recorded in the 3 July 1931 Edition of "Vote" reporting on the 7th Annual Conference of the British Commonwealth League, which had taken place the previous month. The timing of this report is of significance, not only personally due to Ivy's own experiences from the Hague Conference, but also as 1931 represented perhaps the nadir of the extreme financial hardship felt in Great Britain after the war. This, in turn, made questions of inheritance and the entitlement of women to inherit of greater importance. The way in which this report is recorded in the minutes of the conference is perhaps telling. Most discussions and papers were recorded in great detail, with interjections from the floor reported verbatim. Ivy gave a paper on the English law position (and that of the Dominions) on the law of inheritance as it affected women; she was followed by two further papers by women on that law as it affected Hindu and other religions. The record of the papers states only that the papers were "*highly technical*" and very interesting but that it would be wrong to try to minute them for fear of getting anything wrong. A condensed version of the papers is said to be available upon payment of a fee. In short – it left the audience cold. It suggests a highly intellectual knowledge –based lecture as opposed to the political opinion –based papers otherwise delivered. Ivy's forte was academic law, not the wider field of political opinion. Quite possibly, on this occasion, she misjudged her audience.

Perhaps surprisingly, when the British Commonwealth league focussed specifically in 1932 on Women's nationality and the effect of marriage – Ivy's specific interest from her involvement at the Hague – the paper was presented by Helena Normanton, and Ivy's participation in this conference was not recorded. By 1932 however, she had moved on to other Governmental work, which may have left her insufficient time to attend the conference.

Chapter 12
Membership of the Aliens Deportation Advisory Committee 1932.

Shortly after her work in the Hague, Ivy returned to public work. In 1921 she had been asked at the time of her call to the Bar when she thought that there would be women judges. Her reply was typically conservative and thoughtful. *"Not for a long time"*. This reflected not only the catch up that women had to do but the typically long period between admission as a barrister and eventual elevation (for a very few of the cream of the profession) to the judiciary.

However, in 1932, Ivy was effectively entrusted with a quasi –judicial appointment, quite possibly reflecting another first for women in the law.

In the period between the wars, an advisory deportation committee was set up as a successor to deportation advisory committees that had sat during the course of the war. This was perhaps in response to the existence immediately after the first world war of perhaps 5,000 former enemy aliens in the country who had expressed a wish to remain but who faced potential expulsion. It was the first such peacetime committee and was set up as a precaution against criticism of the Home Secretary for any apparently "arbitrary" decisions in respect of cases referred to him for deportation. Many of the potential deportees were long –standing residents who had married English women and whose sons had fought with the British in the war. The sheer numbers were overwhelming. On 5 August 1914, The Aliens Restriction Act was passed, requiring aliens to register with the police pending deportation, internment or release. An early advisory committee had been established to advise the Home Office and to reduce its workload, but this had been de facto disbanded with the dissolution of Parliament in 1919. It was re –established subsequently after the enactment of the Aliens Restriction (Amendment) Act of 1919.

In February 1932, an announcement was made that Sir Herbert Samuel (the then Home Secretary) had set up an advisory committee on deportation

> "to advise upon the cases of aliens in respect of whom the Home Secretary has made or contemplates making a deportation order on any grounds other than landing in the United Kingdom without permission or failure to observe conditions imposed on landing in the United Kingdom".

The warrant for the formation of the committee was dated 29 February 1932.

The process for the selection of the committee was interesting. The Home Office considered that there should be a spread of interests represented, and on balance, that there should be no sitting MPs as that would require balance with an appointment from all parties. The committee was to be small and able to act quickly and to meet at short notice in London. They would be unpaid, although expenses would be met. It was thought they would review about 20 cases a year. The number of five members was hit upon (although subsequently six were chosen), with a quorate of three. The chair was thought to be a suitable position for a QC or senior lawyers, and early candidates were Lord Blanesborough (a Court of Appeal judge whose Scottish residency and Court duties may have made him unsuitable), CA Lowenthal (or whom no details are available), Roland Vaughan Williams (ultimately selected) and Herbert du Paig KC (a leading lawyer of whom no details are available)

It was also considered necessary that there be a businessman on the committee, and Mr Brand, the director of Lazards, was proposed. A letter of invitation was sent to Mr Brand, and it was assumed that he was unable to accept. The subsequent appointment of Colonel Samuel may have filled this criterion in the event.

An "IU" representative – by which I take this to mean a representative of the unions – a Mr A Pugh and a Mr Rhys Davies were proposed, neither of whom were eventually included on the committee. Arthur Pugh was at the time active in the British Steel Smelters association, and Rhys Davies was an experienced trade unionist but by 1932 was a sitting Labour MP, which would have disqualified him.

The appointment criteria also required that there be "a Jew" on the committee, and the original name nominated was Mr Otto Schiff. Otto Schiff was a noted Jewish philanthropist who devoted much of his life to aiding Jewish refugees – he was credited with saving large numbers of Jews from Germany in the first world war and had served in the British army. In 1933 his focus was on assisting and supporting Jewish refugees, and he may not have had adequate time to devote to the committee.

The committee also (radically) thought it appropriate to have "a woman" on it. There were two initial proposals, Mrs E D Scim (or Scion) and Ivy (who was the second on the list). The first named woman's name is hard to read, and unfortunately, at the time of writing, I can find nothing about her to measure her against Ivy.

150

In other correspondence, the importance of having some candidate recognised by the British Labour party was felt to be of importance. Proposals were unanimously in favour of J J Mellon JP, and they also suggested Major Herbert Evans (whose pending candidacy as MP made him less appropriate) and a solicitor who regularly acted for aliens – W H Thompson. The candidature of the labour representative was said to be something on which the home office wanted the blessing of Miss Bondfield. Her name is mentioned several times as being of significant influence in the composition of the tribunal from Labour's point of view. Miss Bondfield is almost certainly Margaret Grace Bondfield (1873 –1953), a British Labour politician, trade unionist and women's rights activist; the first woman cabinet minister and first woman privy counsellor (she had recently been in place as minister of labour) and first woman chair of the Trades Union Congress.

Another potential appointee invited was Professor Zimmern (Sir Alfred Eckhard Zimmern), an English classical scholar, historian and political scientist specialising in International relations. He contributed to the founding of the League of Nations Society and to UNESCO, for which he was nominated for a Nobel peace prize. He was a member of the British Labour party and had been a Labour candidate, a close friend of Ramsey Macdonald – it may well have been his refusal of the offer that led to the search for a Labour preferred candidate.

Of Ivy's candidature, the Home Office does not seem to have had a great deal of information about why she was proposed, and it is a Mr Newsam (later Sir Frank Aubrey Newsam – a leading civil servant of his time) of the Home office who clarified the reason for her potential inclusion in the committee writing on 18th of April, 1931-

"Miss Williams is a doctor of law and holds an appointment as a teacher of the law to home students at Oxford. She acted as one of the British delegates at [the Hague Conference] and possesses a very sound and balanced judgement[30]"

– his words were to be added to all mentions of Ivy in the appointment process.

The committee was intended to be little more than an advisory body with no real powers, to draw the fire away from the Home Secretary and to be "window dressing" for the process. In fact, they were ultimately comprised of 6 serous minded individuals and headed by a KC who would not be whitewashed by Whitehall.

As a result, the ambit of the role that the committee was to play was reduced in scope, and the number of cases that came to it was never substantial. Questions were asked in parliament about why it was even thought necessary to have such a committee to undertake work previously done directly by the Home Secretary. The Home Secretary at the time was able to reply that it was his predecessor who had set up the scheme.

Offers went out to the various selected members on 22 February 1932, and Ivy's acceptance was immediate, replying on a modest headed notelet from her home then Staverton Road, a typed and very brief acceptance signed in a fine nibbed fountain pen in blue ink.

The committee set up was eventually comprised of a number of highly distinguished figures, all familiar with public service and the work of boards and committees. Ivy was in the company of establishment men with a similar

---

[30] For which read "safe pair of hands – unlikely to rock the boat"

educational and political background to her own and with a liberal approach to the world.

The members were: –

Mr Roland Vaughan Williams (KC) Chairman. From a distinguished legal family, Mr Vaughan Williams was the Cardiff City recorder; however, he was selected for his brilliant command of languages and the post –war work he had already undertaken in providing specialist translation services in the delicate work of readjusting the borders of Europe after the war. He was a member of the Anglo –German Mixed Arbitral Tribunal set up under the Treaty of Versailles and thus presumably was felt to be of potential usefulness in the case of the anticipated German nationals who might seek to remain in the country after the war. He chaired the committee.

Brigadier –General Sir Wyndham Deedes – former chief secretary to the Palestine government.

Captain Oliver Lyttleton (subsequently Viscount Chandos) was an energetic businessman who was engaged in metal trading and had contrived strategic plans to protect Britain's metal industry in the event (as came to pass) of war; later to enter politics and to become President of the Board of Trade.

Mr James J Mallon Warden of Toynbee Hall, Whitechapel. Mellon was similarly a distinguished committee person; he became governor of the BBC after his time on the committee and held an LLD from Liverpool university. He had been the secretary of the Anti –Sweating League – a reforming campaign to alleviate the poor conditions endured by many workers in sweatshops, and who called for a minimum wage to be included in the legislation. He was a member of 13 of the first Trade Boards established under the 1909 Trade Board Act, was Honorary Secretary to the Trade Boards

Advisory Council, treasurer of the Workers Educational Association, a member of the economic advisory council of the Industrial Court, chair of the London council for Voluntary Occupation during Unemployment, a member of the Royal Commission on Licensing and member of various committees appointed under the Profiteering Act.

Colonel F D Samuel – Col Samuel was a director of the banking firm of M Samuel and Co and treasurer of the Jewish Board of guardians, and Honorary Secretary of the Soup kitchen for the Jewish poor

Dr Ivy Williams – England's first woman barrister, lecturer at Oxford University and former technical delegate to the Hague on behalf of Great Britain.

The membership was philanthropic and international in its outlook, on the whole liberal in its politics, and balanced as to its attitude to German nationals. It was necessarily from the monied classes as the members were unpaid. As a committee, it seems to have had only a limited workload – it only sat when cases were referred to it by the Home Secretary.

The committee first met on 17 March 1932 when it drew up its rules of procedure; these included restrictions on evidence and requested the provision of a shorthand note –taker (in fact, no notes exist of the cases considered – only summaries) and the use if required of an interpreter.

In the event, the committee were to sit 14 times between 1932 –1933[31] where after there is no record of their

---

[31] Sittings
24.5.32 Agreed to deport Belovitch, Dahit, Goldghei and reserved two pending more information – Poli and Winfield. [William Winfield and William Unwin in July 32 a note was circulated to the committee as a law-abiding man in work cannot be said to be not conducive to the public good.]
16.6.32 Suggested not to deport Winfield and Poli, but to deport Martin. Ivy did not attend this meeting.

meetings. The committee still existed in 1936 and was under review in 1937, but the only record of these later dates is that the Home Office was in discussion with the chairman to reduce the ambit of the committee's work, which they seem to have ceased altogether.

Ivy attended all but two of the meetings; very few were attended by all members, and the chairman was always in attendance. There is evidence that they did come under political pressure to "rubber stamp" the orders to deport that they were considering. This they resisted quite regularly. Of the 23 cases that came before them for which records still exist, 9 were either refused or in some other way returned. They upset the Home Office by requiring first –hand evidence of why the deportation order was sufficient and was not content to rely on a written "brief" from the Home Office, asking to hear from arresting officers so as to establish the facts of the matter – it seems that they had never been intended to be a fact –finding tribunal, and this approach may have hastened their demise. Regularly they were treated as some form of appeals tribunal and not simply an advisory body, and

---

14.7.32 Agreed not to deport Urwin, Ivy did not attend.

14.10.32 Agreed to deport Ceresa but not Impey

6.12.33 Deport Helsgaun

11.1.33 Deport both Solberg and Melihoff

21.1.33 Deport Hartzell

14.2.33 Not to deport Holslag

7.8.33 Not to deport GamBardella or Narcisco

10.4.33 deported Lam and ToYit – Lamb had QC

11.5.33 After very lengthy hearing deported Mark and Solomon Wulkan

13.6.22 Advised to enforce deportation order against Wilhelmine Gisella Wildeisen or Clarke

28.7.33 Not to deport Hardter who had counsel

5.12.33 Not to deport Minchella

counsel and leading counsel often appeared (with a measure of success) before them.

Tantalisingly there exist minutes of the various hearings of the committee, but they are Delphic and record only the length of the hearing, the representatives of the parties and the outcome. It is hard to distinguish any individual voice from the committee. On one occasion only is there any sign that Ivy may have been of particular influence in the decision of the committee. This was the case of To Yit – a Chinese who did not contest deportation but expressed concern for his children in China who were in the care of the authorities. A note was added to the finding that whilst the deportation was approved as it seemed implicit that the man would return with his children, their welfare was flagged up as of paramount concern.

Surprisingly it was not the case that – perhaps as anticipated when set up that the committee had to consider cases of German or at least European aliens – the two most celebrated cases of the limited number that came before the committee concerned an Iraqi and an American. These two cases both resulted in the committee recommending deportation (and in the case of the Iraqi facing an appeal through an application for a writ of habeas corpus on grounds inter alia that the committee had exceeded its powers and acted in an unfair manner. That application failed).

Hansard for May 1936 records a question about the members of the committee and the number of cases awaiting its decisions. The reply came that the committee comprised the original members and that it had most recently sat on the 4,5 and 19 December 1935 when they had considered the cases of 7 aliens (no record of the 1935 sittings now exists) and had had no further cases referred to them. After this time, the committee was disbanded.

156

Chapter 13
Later life.

After 1936 Ivy seems to have settled for a quieter life and to have enjoyed the company of a close –knit circle of friends as well as her work at the university. There is no record of any wartime activity in the second world war, although, with the removal of many of the governmental departments to Oxford and the conscription of male students, the demographics of college life will have changed significantly. In 1939 She was living at 30, Staverton Rd with Nora MacMunn (b 1875) (retired Oxford tutor) and Alice Rylance (b1871) (retired missionary), and housekeeper Ina Terry – all single women. Ivy was still working as a tutor, having ended her work on the Aliens Advisory committee. She worked as a tutor until 1945, and her retirement aged 68. Immediately prior to her retirement, she contributed to the acquisition of 11, Bradmore Road, which was to be renamed St Anne's House and to provide additional student accommodation for her college (before eventually being sold to Kellogg College). She enjoyed over 20 years of retirement during which little is known apart from the fact that she became blind and her health – always a matter of concern to her – also deteriorated. With the realisation that she was losing her sight and unimpressed with the state of reading material for the blind, characteristically practical, she developed her own Braille primer in 1948, which went into several editions through the National Institute for the Blind. Blindness ran in the family, and I recall my great aunt Cordelia ("Corrie") Prior bringing with her to a stay in Maidenhead extremely large and heavy volumes of Braille books sourced for her by Ivy.

In 1956 she was made an honorary fellow of St Anne's. She died on 18th February 1966 at 30, Staverton Road, attended by her housekeeper Ina, the cause of death was given as coronary insufficiency, atheroma and osteoporosis. She was cremated and her ashes scattered at the Oxford crematorium at Headington; no stone marks her existence. The local newspapers did not mark her passing.

Who were Ivy's friends in her later years? Some assistance here can be gained from the terms of her will – the last version of which she made in 1962, which indicates those most important to her in those later years, although as a practical person, she gifted monies to those she deemed most in need so exclusions for example of certain of her cousins who were financially secure should not be taken to be an indication of lack of affection. The will was made in 1962, but by the time of her death, one of the beneficiaries had already died.

Ivy's will left bequests neatly categorised between friends, family and helpers.

It is a simple will[32]. It appoints an executor and a fallback; it appoints solicitors, and it applies cash for the maintenance of her mother's grave in Highgate cemetery in perpetuity (although correspondence with the guardian of Highgate cemetery reveals that for some reason – perhaps the estate did not have sufficient funds to give – no funds were applied at all to the upkeep of the grave but that it was instead transferred as to ownership to Ivy's

---

[32] The will is attached as an appendix

executor. Fortunately, Ivy had selected durable red granite for the headstone, which remains in good condition to this day in spite of no funds being earmarked for its maintenance).

It leaves her braille equipment and desk to the executor, Mary Banbury, a former administrator at St Anne's College, and perhaps herself suffering from loss of sight.

It leaves small bequests to her "cousins", her "friends", and her "friend and helper".

These were: −

"Cousins" − Cordelia and Gladys Prior and Winifred, Janet and Winter Cousins. Winter was the only male beneficiary. By 1960 when the will was made, Ivy had outlived most of her numerous cousins. On her mother's side, she had been close to her uncle Charles (who was her financial advisor until his death) and to her unmarried aunt Rosa who had died twenty years previously. She seems to have lost touch with her uncle Thomas's family, but it is surprising perhaps that she did not think to leave anything to her cousin Florence who was still alive in 1960. Florence was Charles Ewers' daughter and in 1911 was living with her parents in Oxford (having been born in Sheffield) employed as an Elementary School teacher; by 1939, she was living with her housekeeper Elsie White having retired as a head teacher living at 68, Hill Top Road in Oxford which was to be her home until her death in 1962.

On her father's side, she had numerous relatives spread across the globe. A number had, however either remained in Oxford or had returned there. All her aunt Eliza's children, had predeceased her, although there is little indication that the Bakers and the Williamses were particularly close. Her uncles Henry and John remained in her thoughts as the support she sent to her uncle during her lifetime illustrates, but it was to her two aunts Martha Wallis and Mary Abigail 's families, that Ivy seems to have been closest.

Mary Abigail had married a renowned missionary and had had a number of children, all of who had died by the time Ivy came to write her will however, Herbert Cousins, Mary Abigail's son, had been a senior civil servant in Jamaica doing important work to build the agricultural department in Jamaica. He had three children, Winifred, Janet and Wilfred. Ivy left bequests to the two girls. They had returned to Oxford after living in Jamaica and lived together at 34, Uplands Park Road in Oxford with their parents in 1939. They seem to be examples of "wonderful Williams women" identified earlier in this work; Janet was a novelist who wrote about the plight of slavery in Jamaica in her three novels. Winifred described herself as an anthropologist and was similarly engaged in anti – slavery and awareness – raising work – and Ivy had been her first referee in her application to Royal Holloway to read for a History degree. They remained unmarried.

Winter was the son of Arnold Cousins, and his family originated from South Africa. He travelled extensively as a civil servant and visited Great Britain on a regular basis. Whilst it is likely that Ivy kept in touch with him, it is hard to imagine that there was a particularly close relationship, and my belief is that she honoured his parents' decision to retain the family name and wanted to express her love for her brother through this bequest to her nephew. I could, of course, be entirely wrong, and there could have been a close relationship, but geography is against it.

Ivy's aunt Martha was the youngest of her father's siblings. She married Harry Neville Prior and had six children, of whom three were still alive in 1960. Ivy gives her address in the St Anne's records at one stage (tantalisingly undated) as Highfield, which was the large house built by the Priors. Of these two girls – Cordelia (Corrie) and Gladys were unmarried and living together very simply and quietly in Hazels in the Headington quarry area of Oxford with their brothers Percy (until his death in 1956) and Sydney (who died in 1952). The house was a basic bungalow with little adoration (the plasterboard was unfinished), and Cordelia looked after it and the garden. Percy had a modest practice as a solicitor (strictly no advocacy as he was of a retiring nature), and Gladys is referred to from time to time as a farmer and had earlier lived close by in a smallholding; at another stage, she is registered as a masseuse. All the siblings had investments from inheritances which they lived on very quietly. They had a man who helped them from time to time. The house at Hazel's caught fire in the early 1960s, and it is there that the papers relating to Ivy's business affairs (and indeed those of her father) were kept; most were lost. The few that survived were taken to Robin Silvio Prior's house in Maidenhead, where they were never reclaimed, and the few remaining – Percy's letter book and George St. Swithin Williams's account book – are now in my possession.

Other cousins did exist but were not included in the will. My grandfather Robin for example, certainly knew Ivy but whose business had started to thrive and had no need of her assistance. Also, still alive were various nieces and nephews

Her "friends" are listed as Nora E MacMunn, Nancy Hopkins and Elsie Abbiss.

These were her long –time friend and sometime housemate at Staverton Road, Nora MacMunn, a former geography teacher at St Anne's and militant suffragette. Nora had shared a house with her, her housekeeper Ina Terry and retired missionary Alice (Maud) Rylance in 1939.

"The Ship"[33] records in her obituary:

> *"Miss MacMunn lived for many years in her much –loved rooms in 5, Bath Place[34], where her students were always welcome. She spent many long vacations in the South of France and Switzerland. She was a close friend of Dr. Ivy Williams, and was much interested in her work on books for the blind, herself learning to read Braille by touch. From Bath Place she moved first to 196, Banbury Road[35], and then, with Miss Maude Rylance[36], to Horseshoe Cottage near*

---

[33] The periodical of St Anne's College
[34] This address is now occupied by the Bath Place Hotel, it is a beautiful little 17th century enclave.
[35] This address is quite close to Ivy's house at Staverton Road
[36] Alice (Maud) Rylance was a retired missionary and a little older than the others. She had worked in India and records show her departure on one such mission on 27 February 1919 sailing on the "Nagoya" to Bombay (first class).

Andover, where many of us were privileged to visit her. In her old age she moved to Miss Sybil Notley's house in Eastbourne[37]. "

Nora MacMunn was born in Chelsea in 1875, so she was of a similar age to Ivy. Her mother, Charlotte was treasurer of the St Leonards Women's Suffrage Propaganda League, and both Nora and her sister Lettice were also on the committee. She was a chaplain's daughter. She was educated privately before joining the Society of Home –Students at Oxford, where she took a third in modern history in 1903 and the Oxford Diploma in Geography in 1904. She was appointed a demonstrator in Geography by A J Herbertson in 1906 and lectured in Geography between 1909 and 1935 – holding a junior post. Like Ivy, she took her degree in 1920.

Nora devoted herself to a lifetime of radical feminism. She joined the Oxford Women's Suffrage Society and marched with them into London in 1908. She was also a member of the Oxford branch of the Women's Social and Political Union ("WSPU") – this was a leading militant organisation campaigning for women's suffrage in the United Kingdom between 1903 and 1918, its members became known as the suffragettes, and its membership was tightly controlled by the Pankhursts. The members

---

She may well have been a contact of the Cousins. She predeceased Ivy dying in Eastbourne (like Nora) in July 1959 which explains her omission from the Will.
[37] Probate records give Nora's final address as 30 St John's Road, Eastbourne although she died in the Esperance Nursing home on 14 May 1967; a Sybil Gertrude Notley 1890 –1965 lived at 9 Arundel Road, Eastbourne; in 1939 Sybil and Gertrude Notley (widowed mother) lived at 18 Upperton Road Eastbourne, Sybil is listed as a lecturer and tutor MA Oxon. Born 1889, her father was a merchant and stock broker, and she seems to have spent time in Liverpool and London.

became known for civil disobedience and direct action, heckling politicians, holding demonstrations and marches and causing property damage so as to ensure that they were arrested. Nora is the only known member of Oxford University for whom an arrest warrant was issued as a result of her activities on behalf of the WSPU, although the Geography department was known to have three members amongst its ranks and the Society of Home – Students had five. Nora made monetary contributions to the WPU in 1912, 1913 and 1914 – at a time when Ivy was setting out on her own political career locally. The friendship with Ivy seems to have developed after Nora's period of militancy, and by 1935 she had retired from university life.

Family history indeed recalls Ivy having a holiday house in Ludgershall, which she shared with Nora. This could easily have been Horseshoe Cottage near Andover, referred to in the "Ship", which records show to be a four –bedroom detached cottage thatched with gardens and stables. The address of this cottage is given as Ibthorpe, but it is not far from Ludgershall. I had thought that the cottage was, in fact, more likely to have been in Ludgershall, Buckinghamshire, where there is also a Horseshoe cottage in the High Street. At the time of writing, there is no evidence to rebut the recollections of the students who contributed to the "Ship"; what is a bit surprising is that the house that family recollection is that it belonged to Ivy seems, in fact, to have been a house eventually shared by Alice Rylance and Nora – similarly, suggestions that Nora was in any way a "special friend" of Ivy seem to be gainsaid by the fact that it seems instead to have been Alice and Nora who were especially close.

Elsie Abbiss was, I believe, a university exam marker. No address is given, so it is to be assumed that Mary Banbury knew these people. It suggests a university connection. I believe Nancy Hopkins to be Fanny Hopkins, who was the widowed sister of Elsie Abbiss, both living in Cowley Road in 1939, with a third sister Betty who died in 1943, and a further sister Dorothy Downey. The address in 1939 was 337, Cowley Road, Oxford. It seems likely that Ivy knew the entire household of sisters and that when she came to make her will, she remained in touch with Elsie and Fanny.

Her "helper" is given as Mrs Collett, who gets a lesser bequest. The Collett family were relatives of Ivy's – her great grandfather Peter had married a Collett who is well represented in the graveyard at Cote; elsewhere, there is a reference to a Miss Jackson looking after Ivy's mother in Cote (probably the house at 30, Staverton Road) in the letters' book and also to the fact that Miss Jackson put on weight after Ivy went North to convalesce up until when it seems that Miss Jackson had to wheel her around. Miss Jackson is also referred to as living in Divinity Road (Cowley). Miss Jackson seems to have taken a great pride in looking after Ivy's home and was likely Ina Terry's predecessor and in all probability predeceased Ivy so did not feature in her will.

Her executor was Mary Banbury who was a Home – Student from 1926 –1930 and read geography. She taught briefly at Wychwood school before taking up a post as Assistant Secretary in the office of the Society of Oxford

Home –Students, where she worked until retiring in 1972, she died in 1996. Of interest is the fact that Ivy bequeathed her Braille writing machine, desk and teaching books on Braille, suggesting that Mary Banbury was involved in helping the blind, or was herself losing her sight.

Her residuary beneficiary was her housekeeper Ina Terry and her unmarried younger sister Elsie Margaret Terry. Ina Terry was born in 1902 and died in 1976 in Hampshire. She was part of a large family her father being a corn merchant. Why Ivy left her house to her is unclear. It is inconsistent with bequests in her life to the community or the university, and suggests either a deep affection for her housekeeper or a recognition of a need for her to have the house. The property is now used for graduate accommodation.

Chapter 14
Some thoughts

A suffragette?

Yes and no. No record exists of Ivy's formal affiliation with any women's suffrage group. Her donations to Mrs Fawcett's[38] charities were restricted to her war fund not her political funds. Her absence from the 1911 census (boycotted by suffragettes) may have been a quiet mark of solidarity but equally she may have been convalescing overseas. That she and her family recognised and supported equal rights for women is clear. She speaks of it in her first speeches as a Liberal. That they went out of their way to achieve financial equality for women is reflected in the wills of her grandfather, father and mother. Her friendship with Nora MacMunn – she of a much fiercer temperament and reputation as a suffragette – would not have been possible without similar sympathies. But Ivy was politically prudent. As her speeches to the Hague conference show, she realised that extremism rarely results in success, and that a more measured path is likely to achieve more. Her speech at the Hague was frankly disappointing from a feminist point of view suggesting that women are somehow inevitably

---

[38] Millicent Fawcett was one of the leading campaigners for women's suffrage and legal change and between 1897 –1919 led the National Union of Women's Suffrage Societies

driven to act in a certain way. Like many of us the flame that burned brightest in youth dulled but was never extinguished. The logic of her declaration of 1924 that

> "*Ladies holding University law degrees, learned and skilled in the law, deservedly enjoying public confidence, could legally compete in vast fields of solicitor's and counsel's most lucrative domains and without infringing the law*"

– which to us today seems unassailable, was never lost when, at her call in 1922, what may seem to others to be a withdrawal from the fray was actually another battle cry when she stated that whilst she herself would not practice that she would prepare girls for the exams and that "*they will practice*". She became an enabler when she was originally set on a course of pioneer; her whole life was dedicated to the service of her community and to the women in particular. A suffragette? Of course. In the widest possible sense of not just seeking political enfranchisement but the opening of all opportunities to women.

Romance?

Ivy died a spinster. There is no suggestion that at any time in her life she was romantically attached to any one person. There are perhaps though a few small indications of an emotional relationship. Nora MacMunn has frequently been linked to Ivy as a potential love interest. They certainly spent time together and the "Ship" noted that closeness. I suspect they shared a great deal in common as early Oxford women academics, but I doubt it was anything more than a friendship. Many women to the forefront of the legal world at the time seem perhaps to have preferred the company of women and Ivy was cloistered in an all –woman academic environment that suited her nature very well. However, the main reason that I believe Ivy and Nora to have been friends first and last is that whilst in 1939 Ivy, Nora, Ina (her housekeeper) and a slightly elder retired missionary Alice Rylance were sharing Ivy's home at Staverton Road, Nora retired to live not with Ivy, but with Alice.

Ivy was perfectly comfortable in the presence of intellectual men. She worked very well on committees, and was clearly seen as a safe pair of hands by the government in the 1930s. I wonder if perhaps she held a torch for Professor Geldart. She wrote warmly of him in her introduction to the "Sources of the Swiss Code", and even many years after his death paid tribute to him. He was of a similar age to her, and although married, the marriage had no children. We shall never know.

Jurist or translator?

As a lawyer Ivy valued clarity and precision. She described her Bar tutor Cuthbert Spurling as a "*marvel of clarity*" – highest praise. That clarity expressed itself most obviously in her linguistic skills. She spoke many languages; her Russian was of such a level that she was able to collaborate with a leading Slavonic scholar to produce a translation of the work of Garshin in 1920; at the Hague in 1930 she addressed her audience in French and her appointment to the Aliens Committee was in part due to her work on the Swiss Code required translation from three languages. From the work that remains it is difficult to judge her skill as lawyer other than to say that she "explained" through translation the work of others. Her "Sources" of course are more than a translation but again they are an account rather than an analysis – although her knowledge not just of the origins of the Swiss code but of other codes (she frequently cites the French Code and German jurists) is impressive. In short many of her achievements owe more to her language skills than her skills as a black letter lawyer. But who can deny the success at the Bar finals (although having taken those exams myself I venture to suggest that after a lifetime of scholarship and practical application during the war, the exams may have seemed rather simple.). That Ivy was a confident public speaker from an early age suggests that even though in the event she leaned heavily on her language skills, it is likely that she would (as Ruth Deech suggests) have been a highly successful lawyer had she had the opportunity as a young woman.

Cousin Ivy.

In putting together this book in which, as it evolved, even the tiniest scraps of new information were seized upon as deepening my knowledge of cousin Ivy I think I came to know her a little and to recognise family traits in her that I see in other family members. I am the only lawyer of my generation in the family, but my son is following in my footsteps. My youngest son shows in his passion for social justice the spirit that George St. Swithin engendered in his children. My grandfather's respect for education and learning sprung from the academic life of his near relatives.

When I started this journey, I expected to find a blue stocking with prim ideas about alcohol and self –

improvement. How much more I found. A woman ready to go into the world on equal terms, a doer as much as an enabler, a formidable intellect. And as I delved deeper I learned that the story would never completely be told – whilst Ivy clearly wanted no fuss and her executor quietly disposed of her papers, still a remnant remained. And with today's significant access to documentation there is rarely a day when some new scrap of information doesn't surface which in its turn leads to a new discovery and different perspective. Ivy I'm only just getting to know you.

A footnote

The gene pool; genealogy

Ivy's family history perhaps throws some light on how she came to have that crucial mix of intelligence, confidence, determination, sponsorship and luck.

With a name like Williams the instinctive assumption is that Ivy or at least her family hailed from Wales. Of course, there is a Welsh link but so remote as to be very diminished and fully diluted with the blood of the home counties – and touched by family legend. On her father's side the last Welsh based ancestor was John Williams born 1630 – her 5th great grandfather, but her wider family had already ties with Oxford prior to his birth.

The Williams family had lived in or around Oxford for many generations rumoured to have come to the area in the time of Oliver Cromwell when two (or possibly three) brothers arrived from Brecon, forced out by religious persecution, and settled in Shifford and Cote. Legends tell of how the brothers arrived tired and dusty from a long journey east and selected Shifford as their new home and went on to prosper there as farmers and landowners. There is rumour of them driving their sheep from Wales and that they first stopped their (doubtless extremely weary) flock in the parish of Bampton at a place along the Witney Mile known as Welchman's Gap, and there made it their home. There is more contemporary evidence for this story. The Aston Near Bampton parish register for the year 1838 contains a postscript to the effect that the registrar (the vicar Richard Pryce who was the Coate minister between 1819 and 1840) wanted to register retroactively the births of the four children of William Williams, grandfather Adin's brother. He justified this as *"the names belong to an ancient family who came from the Principality almost three centuries ago and settle in the vicinity"*. The Aston History Group published a history of the parishes of Aston, Cote, Shifford and Chimney in 2021. This included references to the Williams family and contains a sketch of the Williams brothers arriving in the vicinity and throwing a straw into the air and letting providence guide them – which it duly did to Bampton.

A more likely story is that the relationship between the Williams of Brecon and Shifford was established through marriage in the 16th century. Ivy's seventh great uncle was Sir David Williams. He was the third and youngest son of Gwilym ap Jphnychan (also known as William Williams). The family were well off – yeomen of Blaennewydd in

Ystradfellte, Brecknockshire – and Gwilym' cousin was the historian Sir John Price[39]. Like his descendants Sir David chose the law as his profession and was called to the Bar by Middle Temple on 10 February 1576. He was successful and prosperous in his career and served as recorder for Brecknock from 1587 –1604. From 30 June 1581 –15 August 1595 he was the Queen's attorney general in the court of great sessions for the counties of Carmarthen, Cardigan, Pembroke, Brecknock and Radnor, and argued before Star Chamber. He was called to serjeant –at –law on 29 November 1593, where after his practice extended to Westminster. He was also MP for Brecknock for 4 sessions of parliament. Sir David was knighted by James 1 shortly after his accession to the throne and became a Kings Bench judge. Certain complaints were made of his leniency in allowing relaxed forms of oath –taking, a foretaste perhaps of the non – conformist descendants who would follow. He subsequently became a chancery judge.

His wealth was apparently extensive. He acquired many manors in Brecknockshire, Radnorshire, Herefordshire, Gloucestershire and (significantly) Berkshire.

Sir David's first wife was Margaret, the youngest daughter of John Games of Aberbran in Brecknockshire –

---

[39] Sir John Price also Prise or Syr Sion ap Rhys 1501 –1555 was a Welsh public notary who acted as royal agent and visitor of the monasteries and was also a scholar attributed with the first Welsh printed publication "Yn Ihr vyr hwnn". He was Secretary of the Council in Wales and the Marches, by 1530 he was in the pay of Thomas Cromwell and was a servitor at the wedding of Henry VIII and Anne Boleyn. During the Reformation he was charged with dissolving certain Welsh monasteries and was felt to be mild in his treatment of them, although he seems to have abused his position in taking leases of some of the properties including Brecon Priory in 1537 –38. [ref history.powys.org.uk]

they had nine sons and two daughters, although only four survived; Margaret's older sister Joan was Ivy's 6th great grandmother. His second wife after the death of Margaret in 1597 was Dorothy Wellsborn, who he married on 26 June 1597 when he was 61 years of age. The wedding took place in Kingston Bagpuze – then part of Berkshire, more recently part of Oxfordshire and adjacent to Shifford. Dorothy was the widow of John Latton of Kingston and the daughter and coheiress of Oliver Wellsborn of East Hannay. This second marriage seems to have brought with it the manors of Shifford and Golofers, and the Cokesthorpe estate in Oxfordshire. The records of the Harcourt family suggest that much of the land around Shifford was owned by that family and tenanted, but that the family were in decline by 1769. Shifford Manor is recorded as having been sold in 161 to Sir David Williams who settled Shifford on his second son Thomas (who also acquired freehold land in the area in 1618) who mortgaged it in 1623 to his brother Sir Henry Williams, and then sold a lease and the reversion to Robert Veysy.

Sir David's first wife, Margaret Games (1557 –1597), was the youngest sister (by 21 years) of Joan Games, Margaret's mother was Ann Vaughan whilst Joan's is unknown. Joan also married a Williams – Rogery Williams – and is the more direct ancestor of Ivy, being her 6th great grandmother. Whether Rogery was also related to Sir David is likely, his mother Blanche Vaughan (1504) was possibly related to Sir David's mother Anne Vaughan.

From this it seems likely that the Williams of Brecknockshire's relationship with Oxford and Shifford in particular began in about 1597 when the family acquired land there. Sir David was actually buried (partly) in the church yard at Kingston Bagpuze although the grave has been lost. Milner – Williams in his book on the Williams family expresses the view that in spite of the Welsh connection that there had been Williams time out of mind in Oxford and that they were there before the name Williams came to have any Welsh connection.

Before Sir David Williams the family can trace itself back to Llwyth Elystan Glodrydd the 5th Royal Tribe of Wales of Rhwng Gwy a Hafren ("*Between Wye and Severn*") from around 1000 ad. Ivy's ancestors from the Welsh family include "*Llywelyn of the Big Bald Head*" (about 1200AD)!

In spite of the suggestion that there were always Williams in Oxfordshire the story is that the first direct and permanent relationship with Shifford and Cote amongst Ivy's ancestors seems to have been when John and James Williams, arrived there – it is said – on 1 November 1678. They were Joan Williams' (Nee Games) grandsons. Their father John Williams of Parc ar Irvon had been High Sheriff for Brecon in 1620 and 1654 and was an ardent Royalist. He was Joan's second son, her first born William having fathered five daughters with Blanch Stedman. But John was a controversial character. He was said to have engineered the election of a Royalist sympathiser as MP for Brecon as a result of which on 12 July 1654 "*The Gentry and Inhabitants of the County of Brecknock*" sent a petition to Cromwell and the Council of State which lead to his being outlawed and his lands confiscated[40]. The petition bought to Cromwell seems to

---

[40] The petition (submitted by Henry Williams (doubtless a relative) and Ri Wigmour read "Mr Scobell

We desire you to annex the papers hereto affixed to the petition and certificate formerly lodged with you by us and other inhabitants of the County of Brecknock. And that you will be pleased to present the whole to the noble council of State as soone as you find a seasonable opportunity in order to a sutiable redresse of our juste Complainte. Sir in our absence you will be attended by our Solicitor to knowe the result of the Council thereupon, wee beinge ready to make good the particulars conveyed in our papers. Wee desire your just favour and assistance herein and shall bee ever obliged to remayne Sir your thankful firned and sirvants.

To the right Honourable the Councell of State to his Highness the Lord Protector. The humble petition and certificate of the Gentry Freeholders and nhabitants of the County of Brecon. Humble shewing that according to a writ from his Highness the Lord Protector and his most honourable Council for the free Election of two Knights to serve for this County of Brecon in the next iinsung Parliament to bee held for this Commonwealth of England on ye third day of September next and directed to John AWilliams Esq High Sherrif of this said County who did upon Proclomation and Summond in evidence to the sayd writ assemble ouf selves in the Castel Gorunds of Brecon upon the 12th day of this instant July in all quiet and peaceable manner and without any arms accroidng to a Private Order of Seesions that day proclaym'd for the purposes herein mentoned.

And beng persons qualified according to the Act of this Government of this Commonwealth and diverse ways interrupted menaced and horrified from giving our Votes according to our Conscience & not enjoying a free election according to his highness & his councils Articles therein provided occasioned chieflie by the said Sheriff (not performing (as was concerned) his duty according to the 13th Article) his under sherrif, Bayiffs Jaylor & other Agents being with divers other persons al armed contray to their own Order, who did drag and hold many of the inhabitant to Vote for Mr Edward Jones a person incapable of such Trust according to ye 14th Article being in service against Parliament and a Compounded Delinquent. And notwithstanding our being allowed & thought fit to be a member Competent for ye Part in yr behalf of another Person capable of ye sayd Trust & qualified according to be Publicly names & desires to putt in our just Exepmtins made against divers persons who were in many respects disabled of voting in his behalf & not qualified according to the 18th Article. We were therefore construned both in respect of our duty to God in Obedience to his Highness the Lord Protector his honourabe Concil & the Publique Good to intrust to ur whole County, To declare and Protst Publiquely & unanimously agianst the undercarriage & ye illegal proceedings of the sayd High Sheriff and Edmund Jones Esq & their illegal proceedings, Electon of Edmund Jones Esq continued our protestation against itt & humblie beseeching yo honours n eh Examination of their whole proceedings in the sayd business before he be approved being ready to make just Prooff of all the promises. Submitting ourselves to your hon grace Judgements for our Kindness

176

have been driven by outrage at election fixing and is signed by a group of people, many of whom seem to be his own kinsmen – the Williams and Vaughan families being well represented and potentially ultimate beneficiaries of the lands that were confiscated. The family moved initially to one of Sir David Williams' estates in Gloucestershire (the outlawry was only within Wales) (and a branch of the Williams family continued to reside in Gloucestershire for generations thereafter); from there John and James travelled to the village of Cote in the Parish of Bampton near to which Thomas Williams (grandson of Sir David Williams) had succeeded his grandfather at Cokethorpe Park[41].

There is a slight discrepancy in the dates. The request to exile John is dated 1654, whereas it seems that he first acquired land in Cote in 1648, and thereafter worshiped at Longworth. The brothers put down roots. One married a lady from Longworth which started the Cote/Longworth fellowship. Whilst early meetings were held mainly in Longworth, they started to shift towards Cote over time,

---

herein in what manner shall seem fittest to your Honours for a new & fair Election.

Ever Praying &etc Henry Williams; Edward Vaughan; Richard Herbert; Morhan Jones; John Vaughan; Thomas Vaughan; Robert Walless; Thomas Powell; Roger Vaughan; James Watkins; John Prosser; William Powell; Philipp Williams; James Williams; Richard Winton"

[41] Cokethorpe Park is a substantial house and park near Witney, now an independent school, with a rich and lengthy history. For a relatively short period it was in the hands of the Williams family when Edward and Bridget Fitzherbert sold it in 1610 to Sir David Williams; at this time it was known variously as Golofer/ Giffards and Standlake Fiennes, before being known more generally as Cokethorpe Park. Sir David seems to have undertaken some extension work to the property which was for a while known as Williams' Lodge. He settled it on his second son Thomas who lived there until at least 1623. His son David was married there in 1634 to Elizabeth Carew but sold the property on in 1635. The property is very close to Standlake where in more recent times branches of the Williams family have farmed.

and initially were held at the house of Joseph Collett[42] "*Pond House*"[43] in Cote. John died on 26 October 1693 (of a "*contagious disease*") having married Martha Collett[44]. His third son John married Mary Dale and was selected in 1705 as Trustee for the Cote Meeting. John was Ivy's fourth great grandfather and his son Richard her third great grandfather. By now (Richard lived in Coate or Cote 1671 –1740) the family were well established in the area.

John's brother James was Christened in Bampton on New Year's Day 1674 and lived in nearby Aston, working as a Maltster. He married Mary the daughter and co –heiress of John Williams the Younger of Cote originally from Wick – Risington, Gloucestershire. James had ten children.

Richard Williams, Ivy's fourth great grandfather, married Deborah Dancer and they had several children one of the younger of whom – John (1725 –1801) was Ivy's second great grandfather.

---

[42] Joseph Collett junior married the daughter of John Williams who gave land at Cote upon which the first chapel was built. It was registered for worship in September 1703

[43] Probably Pool House in present day Cote

[44] The Colletts were a well –established local family and on various occasions intermarried with the Williams.

Simplified Family Tree Ivy Williams.

Elysan Glodrydd 950 –1010 married Gwenllian Verch
Einion

I

[12 generations]

I

William Ap Madoc 1515 married Blanch Vaughan

I

Rogery Williams 1540 Married Joan Games

I

John Williams 1600 –1680 married Catherine Meredith
1604 –1700

I

John Williams 1650 –1693 Married Martha Collett 1649

I

Richard Williams[45] 1671 –1740 married Deborah Dancer
1698 –1754

I

John Williams 1725 –1801 married three times, Mary
Selman 1728 –1774

I

Peter Williams 1773 –1857 married Ruth Collett 1777 –
1811

---

[45] Richard had a number of siblings, including one called Adin which seems to
be the first time the name Adin appears in the line; his brother Adin (1692 –
1754) himself had a son called Adin (1714 –).

I

Adin Williams 1803 –1876 married Eliza Bolton 1810 –
1884

I

George St. Swithin Williams 1833 –1904 married Emma
Ewers

I

Ivy and Winter Williams.

Ivy's more immediate family on the Williams side is clearer and a little can and should be said about them and their influence on her life.

Her second great grandfather was John 1725 –1801, his son Peter (1773 –1857) was her (first) great grandfather, (of his son Adin (1803 –1876), her grandfather and his son George St. Swithin Williams, her father much has already been said). All these men (and their families) added to her heritage.

John Williams (1725 –1801). On his death, John's will described him as a farmer and gave his address as Old Shifford (as opposed to New Shifford – there were two farms in Shifford and this was one of them and the more centrally located). He married three times, first to Hannah Collett (the Colletts were a local family with whom the family had previously intermarried; Hannah's father was the pastor at the local chapel) – she was something of an heiress and bought with her "Poole House" (of which there is no current information although from pursuing the Parish history of Aston, Cote, Shifford and Chimney I am inclined to conclude that this is a reference to the property known as Pond House in Cote referred to above) even though she was the third daughter[46]. She died childless aged 23. John then marred Mary Selman with whom he had six children including Ivy's great grandfather Peter Williams; his third wife, Mary Ridge, survived him and bore him a further five children (at least), and dedicated a graceful marble memorial to him (and to her) in Cote Chapel.

His will is long and complicated and was drawn up by the attorneys Leakes whose style is characterised by a tendency to verbosity. He left a considerable estate in terms of the land he owned with property and fields in Cote, Eynsham and Aston. He left land or bequests to all the children of his second marriage to Mary Selman with the exception of his daughter Hannah – his first born. This may have been because he had already made provision for her in her life. Peter received land at Sharps House Close in Aston but subject to him making a payment of £10 to his brother John. As the census subsequently show him residing in Old Shifford that suggests that some rearranging took place of the various bequests left by John. His young son Rowland by his third wife Mary Ridge, who was only 12 at the time the will was made inherited the house at Cote, however he died young in 1823 aged 35 and apparently unmarried after which the farm was acquired by Peter. His children by his third wife shared in the residue of his estate. Of these only 6 have been identified, but that the bequest was substantial is

---

[46] This is corroborated by the 1848 History of Bampton penned by the curate John Allen Giles.

demonstrated by the fact that two of his daughters aged 70 and 81 in 1851 were able to live as "fundholders" and "annuitants" sharing premises. John started fathering children in 1759 when he was aged 34 (his first wife died childless) and continued until at least 1791 when he was 66. He had 14 children. He left his third wife comfortably off in that she was able to endow a graceful marble tablet in Cote chapel commemorating her life – she lived to be 92.

Peter Williams (1773 –1857) spent all his life in the Bampton and Shifford area – he married his relative Ruth Collett on 5 August 1790 and they had ten children before she died (not all of whom reached maturity), including Ivy's grandfather Adin. Although as explained above he inherited land from his father in Aston, following the death of his younger brothers Rowland and Michael he came to inherit the lease for Old Shifford – the ultimate landlords were the Earls of Harcourt. Born in Standlake his mother died within a year of his birth and his father quickly remarried and expanded his family. He seems to have been based in Standlake in the early part of his life and in 1816 he was farming 170 acres of land there as a tenant which land was advertised for rent – the impression being that he was giving up that land. In 1823 he was still based in Standlake as he was acting as a trustee in Bankruptcy for a neighbouring farmer. In 1841 he is shown as residing at Old Shifford as the farmer accompanied by workers. By 1861 some of his sons and their family had moved in with him. Adin was his youngest son and may have felt the confines of Shifford (where the two farms comprised effectively the entirety of the parish) were too great. Little remains to throw light on Peter's influence on his family. He commissioned a chart of the family members but does not seem to have left a will. His obituary described him as "much respected and beloved". Adin seems to have cut ties with him upon his removal to Oxford, the witnesses at Adin's wedding were a member of the Bolton family and Abigail Williams, Abigail was his sister who married a cousin William Talbot Wallis who farmed the other farm in Shifford.

Appendix

Ivy Williams' Will

In the High Court of Justice

BE IT KNOWN that IVY WILLIAMS D.C.L. of 30 Staverton Road
Oxford spinster

died   there   on the   18th   day of   February   1966

domiciled in England

AND BE IT FURTHER KNOWN that at the date hereunder written the last
Will and Testament

(a copy whereof is hereunto annexed) of the said deceased was proved and
registered in the District Probate Registry of the High Court of Justice at
OXFORD

and that Administration of all the estate which by law devolves to and vests in
the personal representative of the said deceased was granted by the aforesaid
Court to MARY BANBURY of 60 Church Way Iffley Oxford spinster

the sole Executrix named in the said Will

and it is hereby certified that an Inland Revenue affidavit has been delivered wherein it is shown
that the gross value of the said estate in Great Britain
                    (exclusive of what the said deceased may have been possessed of or entitled
to as a trustee and not beneficially) amounts to £ 30366 : 1 : 4
and that the net value of the estate amounts to £ 30116 : 0 : 0
and it is further certified that it appears by a receipt signed by an Inland Revenue officer on the
said affidavit that £ 5525 :16 : 0   on account of estate duty and interest
on such duty has been paid.

Dated the 29th day of   April   19 66

Deputy District Registrar.

Extracted by Linnell & Murphy, Solicitors, Oxford

A2

185

This is the last Will and Testament

of me IVY WILLIAMS of Number 30 Staverton Road in the City of Oxford D.C.L., M.A, (Oxford) L.L.D (London) Barrister-at-Law and Hon. Fellow of St. Anne's College in the University of Oxford.

1. I APPOINT my Friend MARY BANBURY to be the sole Executrix and Trustee of this my Will and in case of her death in my lifetime or in the event of her refusal or inability to act in the office of Executor and Trustee then I APPOINT my Friend and Housekeeper INA MARY TERRY to be the sole Executrix and Trustee of this my Will in her place.

2. I DECLARE that in the interpretation of this my Will the expression "my Trustee" shall (where the context permits) mean and include the Trustee for the time being hereof whether original or substituted.

3. I DESIRE that my body be cremated and my ashes scattered in "the Garden of Rest" attached to the Crematorium.

4. I DIRECT that Linnell & Murphy of the City of Oxford Solicitors shall be employed in proving my Will and in transacting all legal business in the administration of my estate and of the trusts hereof.

5. I FURTHER DIRECT my Trustee to pay out of my estate to the Authorities of Highgate Cemetery London (Head Office Nunhead Cemetery Linden Grove Nunhead S.E.15) a sum sufficient for the maintenance of the Memorial and Garden of my Mother's Grave Number 42180 in perpetuity.

6. I FURTHER DIRECT and DECLARE that all estate or other duty (if any) leviable or payable at my death in respect of any property real or personal given or settled by me within five years of my death (or other statutory period then in force) and the interest on such duty (if any) shall be paid and discharged out of my residuary estate.

7. I GIVE and BEQUEATH to the said MARY BANBURY my Braille Writing Machine with its stand and reading desk Together with all my books in or on Braille and all my paper and other accessories for reading writing or teaching Braille Together with my small writing desk in my Study.

8. I GIVE and BEQUEATH the following pecuniary legacies (that is to say) :-

(a)   To my Cousins CORDELIA MARY PRIOR GLADYS MARY PRIOR WINIFRED COUSINS JANET COUSINS and WINTER COUSINS the sum of ONE HUNDRED POUNDS EACH.

(b)   To my Friends NORA E. MACKUNN NANCY HOPKINS and ELSIE ABBISS the sum of ONE HUNDRED POUNDS EACH.

(c)   To my Friend and Helper MRS. COLLETT the sum of TWENTY POUNDS .

9.   I GIVE DEVISE and BEQUEATH (free of all death duties) to the said INA MARY TERRY absolutely (or in the event of her predeceasing me to her Sister ELSIE MARGARET TERRY absolutely) my freehold dwellinghouse and premises Number 30 Staverton Road Oxford aforesaid Together with all my household furniture plate plated articles linen glass china books pictures works of art watches clocks jewellery trinkets clothing and other articles of household domestic or personal use or ornament (save such of the same as may be otherwise specifically disposed of by this my Will or any Codicil hereto) including my wireless sets and the contents of my garage and outhouses.

10.   I GIVE DEVISE and BEQUEATH all the residue and remainder of my real and personal estate whatsoever and wheresoever (subject to the payment thereout of my debts funeral and testamentary expenses) to the said MARY BANBURY and INA MARY TERRY in equal shares as tenants in common absolutely or in the event of the said Mary Banbury having predeceased me the whole to the said INA MARY TERRY absolutely. If the said Ina Mary Terry shall predecease me then but not otherwise I GIVE DEVISE and BEQUEATH the residue and remainder of my real and personal estate whatsoever and wheresoever (subject as aforesaid) to the said MARY BANBURY and ELSIE MARGARET TERRY in equal shares as tenants in common absolutely or the whole to the survivor absolutely if only one shall be living at my death.

11.   SO far as I am legally able I APPOINT GEORGE CLEMENTS of Number 25 Polstead Road Oxford aforesaid to be a Trustee in my place of the St. Swithin Williams' Bequest Trust Fund.

12.   I REVOKE all Wills at any time heretofore made by me
       IN WITNESS whereof I have hereunto set my hand this *fourteenth* day of *April* One thousand nine hundred and sixty-two.

                         Ivy Williams

       SIGNED by the before-named IVY WILLIAMS as her last Will in the presence of us both present at the same time who in her presence at her request and in the presence of each other have hereunto subscribed our names as witnesses :-

J. Maunsend   *W. Drage . S.R.N.*
Solicitor   *Osland Grove .*
Oxford   *Oxford .*

                         2

Acknowledgments

So many people and sources from so many different places have helped me pull together the life of my cousin in time for the celebration of her centenary call to the Bar. It is difficult to list all of them, and doubtless, I will overlook some. But particular thanks are due to Stephanie Jenkins of the Oxford History Society whose knowledge of Headington and Oxford and its people is second to none; to the archivists and librarians of St Anne's College Oxford, in particular Clare White, who were unceasingly polite and patient and who unearthed a valued new photo; to Ruth Deech QC (Hon) for piquing my interest several years ago with a scholarly article and for her kindness and promptness in answering my call that she introduce the book; to Celia Pilkington, archivist at Inner Temple for her freely given guidance and access to records even in the time of Covid and for her wry approach to the facts as presented – sometimes the author cannot see the wood for the trees; to Caroline Morris who first created a significant description of Ivy's life, her account of Ivy's life in "Challenging Women" is far more scholarly than this canter through family history and was truly inspirational; to my aunt Helen Robertson (deceased) for her abiding enthusiasm for family matters and for safeguarding many of the more important artefacts, and indeed for continuing in Ivy's patronage of the Radcliffe infirmary with a further significant charitable gift prior to her death – and finally to the Wordley Partnership for supporting the publication of this book and for recognising its importance in the history of the legal profession and of the example it sets for us still today not just ensuring the access of all to the legal world but for true diversity. In particular to the partners, Paul Wordley and Costas Frangeskides, for affording the project their full and considered support; to Arnas Urbutis, who worked technological magic and finally to my friend Hilary Lissenden, who put her customary polish on the raw text.

All errors are, of course, my own.

Index

Lightning Source UK Ltd.
Milton Keynes UK
UKHW051947230522
403394UK00001B/17